The Complete Beginner's Guide to Tennis

by REX LARDNER
illustrated by Ed Vebell

Here in one comprehensive, clearly written book is all the information a beginner needs and wants to know about the game of tennis. Rex Lardner explains the rules of the game, describes the necessary clothing and equipment, and tells the beginner how and when to execute the basic strokes: the forehand drive and chop, the backhand drive and chop, the serve, the volley, the lob, and the smash.

There are detailed chapters on tactics, the game of doubles (including girls' doubles and mixed doubles), how to get into condition for tennis, how to make the best use of practice time, and how to prepare for a match. The book also features special advice for girl players, valuable tips on how to beat a left-hander, how to use wind and sun to advantage, how to play various court surfaces, and discussions of such subtleties as spin, the drop shot, and the half-volley.

Written for beginners of all ages, this immensely useful guide is illustrated with carefully detailed line drawings and diagrams and is supplemented by a glossary of tennis terms.

THE *COMPLETE* BEGINNER'S GUIDE TO

TENNIS

THE *COMPLETE* BEGINNER'S GUIDE TO

TENNIS

by Rex Lardner

Foreword by Ernest R. Barra

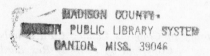
DOUBLEDAY & COMPANY, INC., GARDEN CITY, NEW YORK

Library of Congress Catalog Card Number 67–17265
Copyright © 1967 by Rex Lardner

CONTENTS

FOREWORD

It is my firm belief that of all the sports that boys and girls may take up, they will find tennis the most valuable and very likely the most enjoyable.

The game is splendid exercise. Because of its background and traditions, it teaches courtesy, sportsmanship, and a respect for rules. Since it is a supremely individual sport, it stresses self-reliance; when you lose (at least in singles), you have no one to blame but yourself. When you win, you feel a great deal of satisfaction.

It is a game that requires speed of foot, accuracy, controlled power, deception, stamina, anticipation, and determination. However, if you are weak in one or more of these areas, it is possible to compensate by being strong in others.

The physical benefits of tennis do not end—as do those of many team sports—on graduation. You may not be able to find seventeen other active baseball players when you are through with school, but you can always find a tennis opponent. Throughout school years and long afterward, tennis is the ideal social sport. Players of all ages, boys and girls, men and women, play singles, doubles and mixed doubles, enjoying the thrill of competition.

One of the greatest tennis players of all time, William T. Tilden II, has remarked, "There is no sensation in the sporting world so enjoyable as that when I meet a ball just right." The sensation is shared universally, since tennis is played on nearly every point on the globe: It is popular in Liverpool, Grenada, Rabat, Ankara, Capetown, Reykjavík, Valparaiso, Addis Ababa, Calgary, Munich, and Walla Walla. The top players are known and respected in every city and hamlet in every land. Players of all levels and the sport's millions of devotees find a common bond in their enthusiasm for and knowledge of the game.

Unfortunately, skill at tennis does not come quickly or easily to the beginning player. Sometimes he will feel frustrated because his forehand does not consistently go where he aims it, his serve fails to baffle his opponents, or his backhand seems to involve a whole set of unnatural movements. The remedy is practice and patience, supplemented by lots of competition.

To pat a ball back and forth across the net is easy; to play a good, sound game of tennis is more difficult, requiring a certain amount of self-discipline. Improvement will be faster if you use your time on the court wisely—rallying with a purpose, playing with a purpose, learning from your mistakes, concentrating on your strokes.

As coach of the Huntington, Long Island, High School tennis team* and a constant observer of young tennis players, I have found that the vast majority of young people who take up the game are eager to engage in competition and strongly desire to beat their opponents. This is a healthy attitude and provides a sound motivation for practicing, for seeking the counsel of more experienced players, coaches, and professionals, and for making a study of the game—both on the court and through the printed word.

This illustrated instructional is a valuable guide for beginning players. The author, Rex Lardner, is a long-time student of tennis and has set down, in clear and concise form, the proper ways to hit groundstrokes, the volley, the smash, the serve, and the lob. Such subtleties as spin of the ball, the drop shot and the half-volley are also discussed. There is a detailed section on tactics in singles—how to make the best use of your strong points and how to attack the weaknesses of your opponent. There are chapters on the tactics employed in doubles and mixed doubles, on conditioning and how to make the best use of your practice time—the last two being extremely important, I think, for the player who is

---

* The Huntington High School tennis team accumulated a consecutive streak of one hundred victories from the year 1959 through 1964, winning the Suffolk County league trophies every year during this period—Ed.

dedicated to making rapid improvement. The author also describes tactics for girl players and what you should do when confronted by a left-hander.

This is not a book to be read casually, with the idea that a single perusal will turn you into a champion. Rather, it is a text to be thoughtfully studied, with its salient features recalled and applied when you are actively practicing and playing—and referred to again afterward.

It would probably be advantageous to concentrate on special sections as they relate to what you consider your individual problems—for instance, the serve, the volley, or the smash. Before a match, it might be useful to study the chapters on singles or doubles tactics so that you can make the best use of the weapons at your (and your partner's) disposal.

As far as my own experience in coaching tennis goes, a blanket program that should be helpful to all aspiring tennis champions is: Get in top condition; study all aspects of the game; be receptive to advice from more advanced players; seek out strong competition so that you become aware of your weaknesses; and work seriously to correct these weaknesses. But most of all, play lots of tennis!

Yonkers, New York

Ernest R. Barra

THE *COMPLETE* BEGINNER'S GUIDE TO

TENNIS

CHAPTER ONE

Basic Rules of the Game

The Playing Area: The tennis court is a rectangle 78 feet long and 27 feet wide, divided in the middle by a 3-foot-high net. For playing DOUBLES, a form of tennis involving four players, two 4½ foot-wide ALLEYS are added onto the sides of the court, extending its width to 36 feet.

The interior lines at the sides of the court are called SINGLES SIDELINES; the exterior lines, which form the outside boundaries of the alleys, are called doubles sidelines. The lines at each end of the court are BASELINES. Running parallel to the net on both sides of the court are the SERVICE LINES; each is twenty-one feet from the net. The space on each side of the net between the service lines and the singles sidelines is divided into two equal parts by the CENTER SERVICE LINE. These lines form the four SERVICE COURTS, or BOXES, into which serves are aimed to put the ball in play.

The CENTER MARK is a point in the precise center of each baseline, formed by the imaginary extension of the center service line to the baseline. Its purpose is to let the server know where he is allowed to stand to deliver his serve. Some courts do not have this mark on the baseline, requiring the server to estimate where the imaginary line extending from the middle service line would touch the baseline.

The net is supported by two posts 3 feet, 6 inches high, placed 3 feet outside the doubles court. In important singles matches played on a court used for doubles as well as singles, supplementary net posts are placed 3 feet to the outside of each singles sideline. The height of the net in the center remains the same—3 feet—but with the poles added, the net is slightly higher at the sidelines.

The proper height of the net at the center should always be checked before play by placing one racket vertically on the ground at the net's center point and placing on top of it the frame of another, held horizontally, so that the width of one racket is added to the length of another. Their combined height will provide a fairly close approximation of the 3-foot height the net is supposed to be at its center. A net that is too high or too low can change the entire complexion of the game. In official matches, the height of the net at the center is precisely determined by a special measuring stick.

Singles Rules: The main object in tennis is to hit the ball into your opponent's court in such a way as to make him miss the ball entirely, or to hit the return beyond the court's boundaries, or into the net. A shot that hits the net, or soars beyond the lines, or is missed completely is an error and counts as a point for the other player. A shot that hits the line is considered good.

In competition, play starts with one or the other of the opponents serving. The SERVE is a means of putting the ball in play by tossing it in the air over your head and, as it descends, hitting down on it with the racket—something like hitting a nail with a hammer.

To serve, you stand behind the baseline, positioning yourself between the center mark and the right singles sideline. You must hit the serve over the net and place it in the service court diagonally opposite. If you fail to do this—that is, if the serve lands beyond the lines of the service box or goes into the net—it is a FAULT and your opponent does not play the ball. If it goes into the service box, he must return it over the net and into any part of your court or he loses the point. However, when returning the serve, he must allow the ball to bounce once before hitting it. You have two chances to place the ball in the proper box on the serve. If you fail twice, you have served a DOUBLE FAULT, and your opponent gets one point. If on either serve the ball hits the top of the net and lands in the proper box, the serve is a LET

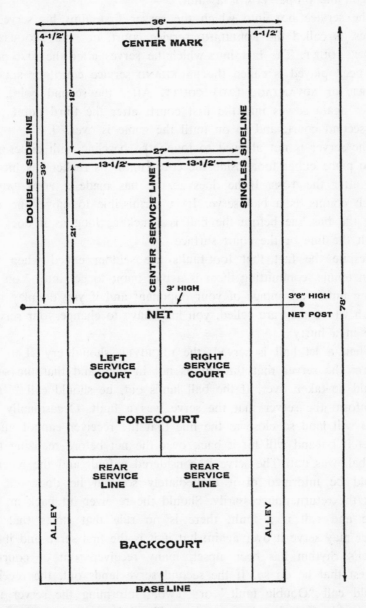

The tennis court: The right service court is also called the first service court, the forehand service court, and the deuce court. The left service court is also called the second service court, the backhand service court, and the ad court. The center mark at each baseline is for the convenience of the server.

and must be taken over. A serve that hits the net and does not land in the proper box is a fault.

The service box into which the server first aims his serve, or serves, is called the FOREHAND service court, or FIRST COURT, or DEUCE COURT. The box into which he serves after the first point has been played is called the BACKHAND service court, or SECOND COURT, or ADVANTAGE (AD) COURT. After the second point, the server again serves into the first court; after the third point, into the second court, and so on until the game is over.

The server is not allowed to touch the baseline with either foot or to place either foot inside the court until his racket has hit the ball after the TOSS. If he does so, he has made a FOOT-FAULT, which counts as a bad serve. It is permissible to move one foot over the baseline before the ball is struck as long as it does not touch the line or the court surface.

Despite the fact that foot-faults are seldom called when you begin tennis, committing them is a bad habit to get into. You are taking unfair advantage of your opponent and if you do play in a match where they are called, you may have to change your serving style in a hurry.

When a let ball is served, the RECEIVER should cry "Let!" to inform the server that the ball is not in play and that the serve should be taken over. If the ball lands out, he should call "Out!" to inform the server that the serve was a fault. Occasionally the serve will land so close to the line that the receiver cannot afford to let it go and will hit it back over the net before realizing that the ball was out. The serve is considered a fault and the receiver should be informed of it immediately so that he does not hit back the return unnecessarily. Should the receiver hit back an out serve and call it a fault, there is no rule that states that the server may serve it over again; but if it is the first serve and if the server's rhythm has been upset, many receivers out of courtesy suggest that he do so. If the second serve lands out, the receiver should call "Double fault," or "Two," informing the server that the double fault has been made. ("Two" is short for "Two bad serves.")

After each game the serve changes hands.

The exchange of shots that takes place after the ball has been put in play is called a RALLY. In rallies, the area between the service lines and the net is called the FORECOURT; that between the service line and the baseline is called the BACKCOURT. During a rally you must hit the ball before it has bounced twice, but it is permissible to hit it before it bounces—that is, on the VOLLEY. You are not allowed to hit the ball before it has crossed the net. Touching the net anywhere—with the racket, hand, feet, or body— is illegal and should you do so, your opponent is awarded the point.

If your opponent hits a ball that looks as though it is going out, let it go. If you catch it before it hits the ground, or if you hit it out or into the net with your racket, or if it hits you (no matter where you are standing), it is technically your opponent's point. The logic behind this rule is that unless you actually allow the ball to hit the ground, you cannot be positive that it would have gone out. It is very poor manners to stand inside the baseline, strike an opponent's shot that might have gone out and shout "Out!" In a case such as this your opponent has every right to claim the point, although he may not do so. A point that, for some reason, should be played over is called a LET POINT.

Before play is started, a racket is spun onto the court by one player and his opponent calls "Rough" or "Smooth"—referring to the way he thinks the slender strings at the top and bottom of the racket HEAD will land. When the side of the racket with the slender strings *over* the gut is up, the toss is SMOOTH; when the side with the slender strings *under* the gut is up, the toss is ROUGH. If the caller guesses right, he has three choices; if he guesses wrong, the spinner of the racket has three choices. The winner's choices are: whether he wishes to serve or receive first; which side of the court he wants to start in; or whether he wishes his opponent to choose first. After one player has made a choice regarding service or court preference, his opponent makes his choice in the remaining category. Thus if one player chooses to serve, his opponent may choose the court in which the wind will be at his back. Or, if one player chooses the court with the sun at his back, his opponent (not wishing to serve into the sun at the outset) may choose to receive.

Courts are exchanged after every odd-numbered game so that one player will not have a decided advantage.

Keeping Score: Tennis scoring is easy to catch onto. No points or zero is called "LOVE"—from the French word for "egg" (shaped like a zero), which is *l'oeuf*. The first point is 15, the second is 30, and the third is 40. The next one—with one exception—is GAME.

The exception occurs when the score becomes tied at 40-all, which is called "DEUCE." (The phrase "40-all" is never used.) Since a game must be won by at least two points, the player winning the first point after deuce is said to have the "advantage." If he wins the next point, he wins the game. If he *loses* the next point, the score reverts to deuce, and each player again tries to win the advantage. After a game has reached deuce, the advantage may go to one player or the other several times before the game is finally won.

Sometimes, for the sake of brevity, 15 is called 5. Thus a score could be called 5-all, or love–5, or 5–40. It is an informal usage, however, and not official. Advantage is often called "ad" in friendly matches, for the same reason. The player whose advantage it is would announce the score as "My ad," while his opponent would refer to that score as "Your ad." Another way of referring to the advantage is in relation to the server and receiver. If it is the server's advantage, the phrase used is "Ad in"; if it is the receiver's advantage, the phrase is "Ad out."

In point scores, game scores, and set scores, the server's scores are always announced first.

Sometimes 30–40 is called "ad out" and 40–30 is called "ad in," the reason being that, as in the case of one player having the advantage (after deuce), only a single point is needed for the game. Thirty-all—because two successive points are needed for the game—is sometimes called "deuce." None of these terms is officially correct, however.

The first point of a game, and points when scores are 15-all,

15–40, 40–15, 30-all, and deuce, are begun in the deuce or first court. When scores are 15–love, love–15, 15–30, 30–15, 40–30, 30–40, 40–love, and advantage in or out, the next point is begun in the second or advantage court. If the score should be, say, 30–15, the next point is always begun in the ad court. By the same token, if the players know that the upcoming point is to be begun in the deuce court, they will realize that the score must be something other than 30–15—perhaps 30-all or 40–15.

When a player has won six games he has won a SET, unless he won his sixth game after the score was 5-all. Since a set must be won by at least two games, he must win one more game, making the score 7–5, to win the set. If the score should reach 6-all, one player would have to take the next two games to win it. Sometimes scores reach nearly astronomical heights, especially in doubles, where service breakthroughs are much less common than in singles. Among the top doubles players, scores of 13–11, 18–16 and 21–19 are not unusual.

A MATCH consists of the best two out of three sets or, in major men's tournaments, the best three out of five.

VASSS: A new method of scoring in tennis which has met with the approval of some spectators and many professional players is VASSS—the Van Alen Simplified Scoring System. This is the invention of Mr. James Van Alen, a businessman and tennis enthusiast who is president of the Tennis Hall of Fame in Newport, Rhode Island.

VASSS dispenses with such traditional terms as 15–love and deuce. Points are counted the way they are in table tennis. A player winning an exchange is awarded one point and the first player to win 31 points—with one exception—takes the match. The exception occurs when the score is tied at 30–30. In this case, since a player must win by two points, the match goes into an eight-point overtime with players serving alternately. If neither player leads by two points at the end of the overtime, another 8-point over-time takes place. As in table tennis, a player is allowed five successive chances to serve, after which his opponent gets five chances. Under this system, long deuce games are eliminated, as are marathon sets. A 31-point match takes around forty minutes to play. (Sometimes the match ends when a player makes 21 points, but most players feel this is too short.)

Doubles Rules: This form of tennis is played with two on a side. The basic rules of tennis prevail for doubles, but the court area is somewhat different. Although the service courts are the same as for singles, after the ball has been put in play by the server, the doubles lines form the side boundaries of the court, giving the players more room in which to hit the ball and also more court to cover.

There is a serving team and a receiving team; after each game they change roles. The serving team consists of a server and his partner. The former serves throughout an entire game and his partner usually plays net. Conventionally, the server's partner positions himself in or near the alley on the side of the court into which the server is serving. After the point is over, the server moves to the other side of the court to serve again and his partner also changes sides. When a serve has been returned by the opponent to whom it was directed, either player on the serving team may hit the ball and either player on the receiving team may hit the serving team's return.

When the game is first learned, players on the receiving team play side by side as service is received; in more advanced tennis, the partner of the receiver will move closer to the net to take advantage of an attacking service return by the receiver. By playing closer to the net he will be able to volley a weak return by the serving team. The player who receives in the deuce court must receive in that court until the set is over, and his partner always plays the ad court. After the set, if the partners wish to switch sides they may do so, but they must continue that way throughout the set.

The service rotates in doubles: the partner of the player who serves first serves the third game; the partner of the player who serves second serves fourth. The rotation of service continues until the end of the set.

If a second set is played, the team that received last serves first in the new set. Either member of this team may serve, after which the normal rotation continues. When their turn comes, either member of the opposing team may serve first.

Occasionally a player will tick a ball with the frame of his racket instead of hitting it—the tick being so slight that he alone knows that the ball has come into contact with his racket. In this case, whether the opponent's shot lands in or out, the player who has ticked the ball and failed to return it loses the point. It is a matter of simple honesty to reveal that the racket has touched the ball and concede the point. In doubles, the situation may arise where one player ticks the ball and his partner, thinking he missed it completely, successfully makes the return. The player who ticked the ball is expected to stop play, explain that he ticked it and concede the point to his opponents.

If the ball is completely missed, however, it is in play until it bounces twice. A player may misjudge a high LOB, miss the ball completely, run back and hit the ball back after it has bounced. This is perfectly legal. In doubles, if one player completely misses the ball, it is legal for his partner to make the return, except on the serve.

CHAPTER TWO

Clothing and Equipment

Proper equipment is of prime importance to the tennis player for both physical and psychological reasons. Tennis shoes that do not fit can cause painful blisters, and a racket that is too heavy or too light can interfere with your stroking. Also, if you are self-conscious about your appearance for one reason or another, you may find it difficult to concentrate on the game. On the other hand, comfortable, practical clothing in traditional tennis white tends to make you feel cool and confident, and undoubtedly helps your game to some extent.

Shoes and Socks: No matter how limited your budget is, do not try to save money by buying cheap, ill-made tennis shoes. Your feet are your best friends on the tennis court and should not be allowed to take abuse. Tennis shoes should fit comfortably over wool socks and should have firm arch support and thick soles for their cushioning value. The shoes should be white, and they should be kept reasonably clean.

Different types of tennis shoes are suitable for different court surfaces. A sole with grooves in it is appropriate for cement or composition courts because it gives the best traction on these very hard surfaces. If you play on grass or clay, however, a relatively smooth sole like crepe is best. This affords good traction and it will not tear up the court as would shoes with grooved soles like the low-cuts worn for basketball on indoor wooden floors. In many cases the court attendants will not allow you to wear shoes with grooved soles on grass or clay courts.

Socks should be of wool to help prevent blisters and to absorb perspiration. They should also be white, not only for the sake of tradition but to prevent infection if you get a cut or blister. If you find that you blister easily or that your feet take an unpleasant pounding on hard surfaces, you should wear a pair of thin cotton socks underneath the wool ones. The two pairs of socks will give your feet better cushioning and protect the skin from being chafed by the friction of the shoes. Socks should be put on carefully to avoid wrinkling, since wrinkles can cause blisters if you are not accustomed to doing a lot of running in the heat. Another method of avoiding blisters on the balls of the feet—where they are most likely to occur—is to cover these areas with moleskin before putting on your socks.

Clothing: Tennis clothes, as mentioned above, are traditionally white. Boys should wear a T-shirt or polo shirt and shorts that are reasonably loose and comfortable. A wool pullover sweater or jacket of orlon, cotton, or nylon is useful for warming up.

The girl's tennis costume should be a form-fitting dress of cotton piqué, cotton duck, or sharkskin, or tennis shorts of the same material and a white polo shirt. The shorts should be short enough and wide enough to permit comfortable and easy movement. A wool cardigan sweater can be worn while warming up.

To keep the sun's glare from hitting directly in the eyes and to provide a measure of coolness, players have their choice of caps, visors, and Australian hats—the full-brim kind favored by Chuck McKinley and Cliff and Nancy Richey. These, too, should be white, though the bottom of the brim is often a cooling green.

Accessories: Since you are bound to do a lot of running in the heat, perspiration may be a problem—on the forehead, the palm of the racket hand, and the face.

It is therefore advisable to take a fluffy white towel with you to the courts. Hang this on the netpost and while changing courts on odd-numbered games make use of it to dry off your face, the palms of your hands, and the racket handle.

If you perspire a great deal, you can buy a sweatband of sponge, synthetic sponge or tarrelin elastic cloth, which fits snugly around the head, preventing perspiration from falling onto the face. Persons who wear glasses may find this accessory particularly helpful in keeping perspiration from dripping down onto the lenses and obscuring vision.

If you wear glasses and find they cloud over when you play on a hot day, you can prevent this by dipping the lenses in cold water before playing and wiping them off thoroughly with a towel or handkerchief.

You can keep perspiration from running down the inside of your wrist and into your palm by wearing a piece of equipment called a Sweatlet. This is a band of elasticized cotton terry cloth that fits snugly around the wrist and absorbs perspiration. Some players wear Sweatlets on both wrists.

The Racket: Most beginning players tend to buy a racket that is too light and has a handle that is too small. With too light a racket you must work harder to hit the ball back, and with too small a handle, the racket is apt to twist in your hand as you follow through in a GROUNDSTROKE. Some stores suggest that the young customer try the largest handle and heaviest racket suitable for his age, and then go to smaller handles and lighter rackets until he finds one that feels exactly right. If possible, it is a good idea to ask a tennis coach or pro to go to the store with you, or perhaps the salesman himself will furnish some sound advice.

Most sports stores and tennis shops use a scale to show the weight and balances of rackets they sell. Beginners, who will play mostly in the back of the court, are advised to get a racket slightly heavy in the head so that the racket will do most of the work when they stroke. It is inadvisable to purchase a "handle-heavy" racket since this cuts down on your ability to "feel" the ball as you meet it.

At the ages of eight and nine, for both boys and girls, the racket should weigh about 12 ounces and the handle should be about 4¼ inches in circumference. Naturally, if you are strong and have large hands, you may want a heavier racket with a larger handle. Try rackets of different weights and handle sizes until you find one that feels right.

For boys between the ages of ten and twelve, the racket should weigh in the vicinity of 12½ and 13 ounces, and the handle should be from 4¼ to 4½ inches in circumference. The girl player's racket should be approximately the same weight, with a handle about 4¼ inches around.

At the ages of 13 and 14, the boy's racket should weigh about 13¼ to 13¾ ounces and the handle should be from 4½ to 4⅝ inches in circumference. A racket for a girl in the same age group should weigh from 12¾ to 13 ounces, and the handle should be from 4⅜ to 4½ inches in circumference. Rackets for older players can go up to 14½ ounces for men, 14¼ ounces for women.

The beginning player is better off using nylon strings rather than gut, though as he improves he may want to switch to the latter. Gut, which is generally more expensive, provides a better "feel" than nylon and gives the experienced player more "bite" in his shots—that is, the ball comes off the racket a little bit faster and spin is imparted a little bit more emphatically. However, nylon usually lasts longer than gut and resists dampness and climatic changes better.

The Racket Grip: A problem many players encounter with their rackets in hot, humid weather is that the grip gets slippery after a few games. A leather grip is best for avoiding this slipperiness, but you may find that even the best grip slides in your hand on a hot, moist day. One solution is to buy a terry cloth grip which wraps around the handle—it has adhesive on the inner side—and gives your palm a nice, firm feeling. The terry cloth grip makes the handle only slightly larger.

Some players who are bothered by a slippery handle—following the lead of squash players, who have been doing it for years— have a specialist in a tennis shop or sports store *reverse* their grips. This puts the rough side out and gives the hand much better traction when the palm perspires, the relative roughness of the grip compensating for the moisture.

Racket Case and Press: It is advisable to obtain a wooden or metal press for your racket to prevent the frame from warping. A racket case is also advisable, to prevent the strings from being attacked by dampness. A canvas case is better than a rubber one, since it allows the strings to "breathe."

Tennis Balls: As much as possible you should use balls that are reasonably new. They are easier to see and more fun to hit since their bounce is consistent. Also, they are less likely to float erratically in the air than old ones, because the fuzz on their surface keeps them on a relatively true course. As the fuzz wears off, their flight becomes less predictable.

CHAPTER THREE

The Forehand

The forehand drive is the bread-and-butter stroke of tennis. It is almost always the first stroke learned, since it is the one that comes most naturally to the beginning player. In the process of developing confidence in this stroke, you will learn the basic principles involved in hitting all the other strokes properly.

These Principles are:
—Watching the ball carefully
—Anticipating where your opponent's ball is going
—Preparing early for the stroke
—Proper footwork
—Firm balance
—A good sense of timing
—Concentration

These are the essential elements in hitting the backhand, the volley, the SMASH, the lob, and the DROP SHOT as well as the forehand. (The serve requires only six of these elements, since your opponent has no control over this stroke.)

Uses of the Forehand: When you are first learning the game, the chief use of the forehand is to keep the ball in play and to develop co-ordination between the racket (as an extension of the arm) and the eye. For safety's sake, your shots should clear the net by several feet. Don't worry if some of them go beyond the baseline. Your object is steadiness and the development of a dependable swing. Later, when the elements of the stroke fall naturally into place, you can concentrate on hitting the ball closer to the net and on placing it in various parts of the court.

As your ability to make use of the forehand increases, you will find it one of the most vital weapons in your tennis armament. It is the stroke with which you can keep your opponent moving from side to side during rallies. It is a dependable means of returning service. When you can hit it extremely well, it becomes a strong forcing shot, driving your opponent back while you take the net. If your opponent comes to the net, your forehand is a means of passing him or causing him to make an error.

Proper preparation is necessary to hit all tennis strokes well. You cannot be casual or lazy in tennis and play a good game; you must move to the ball before you can hit it, and in order to get into position quickly, you must be almost literally on your toes.

The Ready Position: In rallying, you should stand in the center of the court at about the baseline, the racket gripped in your right* hand and pointing toward the net so that you will be able to turn it easily to the right or left as your opponent's shot dictates. The THROAT of the racket should be supported by the fingers of the left hand. This relieves the right hand of some of the weight of the racket and it also allows the left hand to initiate the turn of your shoulder to the right or the left as the racket is brought back in preparation for the return.

Your weight should be on the balls of your feet, your feet should be about twelve inches apart, and your knees should be slightly bent so that you can move toward the ball quickly.

The Forehand Grip: For the forehand you should use the EASTERN FOREHAND grip. This gives good support to the racket as it swings parallel to the ground in the forehand drive and allows

* While left-handed players enjoy many advantages in tennis and several other sports, most instruction books are written for right-handed people. This one is no exception. If you are left-handed, please substitute left for right and right for left throughout.

The ready position.

you to swing *through* the ball—the objective in all groundstrokes. It also allows you to put natural topspin on the ball—spin that helps keep the ball in court and adds pace to your shot.

To assume the Eastern forehand grip, hold the throat of the racket in your left hand, the frame perpendicular to the ground, the handle pointed toward your body. Then shake hands with the racket with your right hand—that is, place the palm of your hand against the flat side of the handle on the right and curve your fingers around it naturally. The heel of your hand should rest against the heel of the racket handle and your forefinger should be extended along the handle for better control of the racket. Your thumb should lie partly on top of the handle and partly across the upper left BEVEL. When the grip is properly assumed, the face of the racket and the palm of the hand supporting the racket are in the same hitting plane.

Stroking the Forehand: Assume the Eastern forehand grip and set yourself in the ready position. Watch the ball closely as it comes off your opponent's racket. Judging the ball's speed and determining approximately where it will bounce, move into position—that is, move to a point where you can hit the ball at about hip height and far enough away from your body so that the right arm will be almost fully extended as you make the forward swing.

When moving toward the ball, be careful not to get too close to it or your stroke will be cramped. Draw the racket back as you move so that you will not have to do this at the last split second. Since you will be swinging forward horizontally, you should draw the racket back horizontally.

The position of your feet as you hit the forehand is extremely important. When you are ready to swing, the right foot should be parallel to the baseline and the left foot—at about a 45-degree angle to the baseline—should be about six inches closer to the right sideline than the right foot. Your feet should be about eighteen inches apart and your weight should be on the right foot. At the conclusion of the backswing your body is sideways to the net, both knees are slightly bent, and the racket has been drawn back so that it is at a right angle to the baseline.

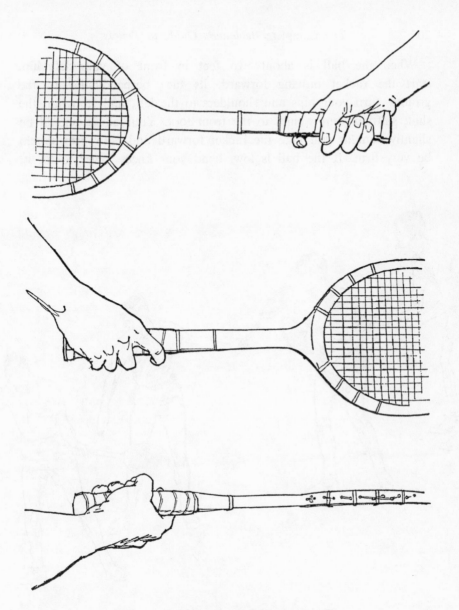

Three views of the Eastern forehand grip.

When the ball is about two feet in front of your left hip, start the racket moving forward, its face perpendicular to the ground, turn your hips and shoulders to the left, and lean into the shot, shifting your weight to the front foot. Your elbow should be slightly bent as you take the racket forward and your grip should be very firm. If the ball is low, bend your knees lower to hit it;

The forehand drive from the ready position to the follow-through

do not drop the head of the racket. When you make contact, try to hit *through* the ball, keeping the racket strings on it for an extra split second before completing your follow-through. If you quickly whip the racket around your body instead of continuing forward with it, you will not achieve the accuracy that you should. TOPSPIN is imparted by the natural forward movement of the arm, wrist, and hand on the stroke; it is a mistake to turn the wrist for extra topspin.

It is very important in hitting all tennis shots to discipline yourself to watch the ball until you see your racket strings make contact with it. Even though you may be tempted to see where your opponent has stationed himself or to look up ahead of time to satisfy your curiosity about the success of your stroke, you must not raise your head abruptly or take your eyes off the ball.

After you have hit the ball, your hips continue to pivot and the racket is brought forward and around in a smooth follow-through, finishing at a point opposite the left shoulder. After making the stroke, you should move quickly to the center of the court and again assume the ready position.

Once you have confidence in the stroke, you will want to place the ball where your opponent has the most difficulty reaching it. To send it to his forehand side, if there is an opening there, hit a fraction of a second *early*. To send the ball down the middle, aim for the middle of the net and at a height that will safely carry the ball over it. To send the ball to your opponent's backhand, hit a fraction of a second *late*.

With practice, you will be able to determine exactly how late or how early you must hit the ball to direct it to the precise spot you want.

The Forehand Chop: This is a stroke somewhat similar to the forehand DRIVE, but the ball is struck down on by the racket and carries BACKSPIN rather than topspin. The CHOP is a useful stroke to learn, but it is by no means a substitute for the drive. Its main function is to confuse an opponent by means of the unexpected spin, hopefully causing him to miss. Topspin (the natural spin imparted on a forehand drive) causes the ball to sink after it crosses the net and to take a long, relatively high bounce; backspin causes the ball to rise slightly after it crosses the net and to bounce nearly vertically after it lands. For hitting a chop, the CONTINENTAL GRIP is more comfortable than the Eastern forehand. Vertical movement of the wrist is easier with this grip and the fingers have more delicate control of the racket. The Continental, incidentally, is also used for the SLICE SERVE, the smash, and the sliced lob.

To assume the Continental grip, hold the racket in front of you as you do for the Eastern forehand grip but instead of shaking hands with it and placing the palm against the flat side of the handle, place the palm over the upper right bevel so that you have the kind of grip you would take for chopping wood with a hatchet. The thumb should lie flat against the flat side of the handle to the left and the forefinger should be extended along the handle for better control.

Another way to assume this grip is to take the Eastern forehand grip and give the racket a slight turn to the right. This has the effect of moving the palm toward the top of the handle. Getting

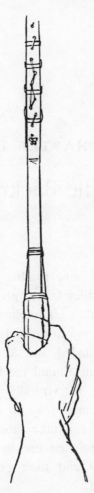

The Continental grip (seen from overhead).

into position, placing the feet, drawing the racket back, and shifting the weight to the back foot are the same for the chop as for the drive. However, because the racket will be swung down on the ball, it is held at about a 45-degree angle to the ground. Your racket hand should be at hip height while the racket head should be at about shoulder level.

When the ball is about two feet in front of your left hip, bring the racket forward and down, its face slightly uptilted, shift your weight forward, and meet the ball. The effect should be one of cutting into the ball and under it. There is almost no follow-through to the chop, the racket stopping at about knee level on the right side of the body.

CHAPTER FOUR

The Backhand

Most beginning players have trouble hitting their backhands—for two basic reasons: (*a*) they fail to get ready for the stroke in time and (*b*) they would rather hit forehands. Their lack of confidence in the shot causes them to run around almost every ball hit to their left if they are right-handed and to their right if they are left-handed. If they can't run around the ball, they are likely to make an ineffectual stab at it, virtually conceding the point. This tendency also causes them to play far over to the backhand side of the court so that they can take most shots with their forehand. Since they avoid shots to their backhand, they never learn how to hit the stroke properly and their potential as tennis players is reduced by at least half.

Uses of the Backhand: Actually, the backhand is a more natural stroke than the forehand. The swing from that side gives the arm and hand firmer control over the racket and it can provide equal power. One deals cards backhand. The backhand blow in boxing is illegal because of the power that can be put behind it. A very effective judo chop is rendered backhand. In golf, the club is supposed to derive its greatest power from the arm that is swinging backhanded.

Many of the world's past and present tennis stars would rather hit the ball on their backhand side. Ken Rosewall and Don Budge developed devastating backhands—such powerful weapons that their opponents often directed attacks to their forehands. Aware that left-handers traditionally have weak backhands, Rod Laver developed a powerful topspin backhand that was the scourge of amateur tennis in 1962 and was a major factor in enabling him to win the Grand Slam—the championships of Australia, Wimbledon (Great Britain), the United States, and France. Players of any level find that once they have learned to hit the backhand with confidence, it is often a more dependable stroke than the forehand. Because of this, some players would rather receive service on the backhand and they relish short shots to this side so they can skip forward to the ball, hit it deep and follow it to net.

The main reason that the backhand is a more natural stroke than the forehand is that the body is out of the way of the shot. When the stroke is made properly, the arm moves forward and follows through with great freedom of action and the body uncoils behind it with considerable natural power.

Apart from the positive reasons for developing the backhand, there is the question of self-defense. You *must* have a good backhand when you compete against a strong player. If your backhand is weak or ineffectual, he will pound it until it completely collapses. It is very poor tactics, against a good player, to keep running around the backhand. The maneuver is tiring and it opens up great areas of court on the forehand side. Also, it is most unlikely that the backhand volley can be learned if the backhand drive is neglected, and this weakness invites additional trouble—that is, when you find yourself up at net your backhand side will be very vulnerable. Then, too, there is the psychological pressure you impose on yourself by coming to battle, as it were, only half-armed. Thus, no matter how much discipline it requires, you must develop a strong backhand.

The Backhand Grip: The EASTERN BACKHAND grip is recommended for all beginning players, since it gives excellent support for the racket as it is brought forward to meet the ball on that side. It also eliminates the possibility of a sharply chopped shot—a backhand which undercuts the ball being considered a weak shot, as compared to a flat-hit or topped backhand, in today's tennis.

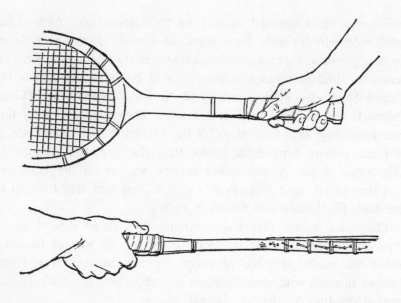

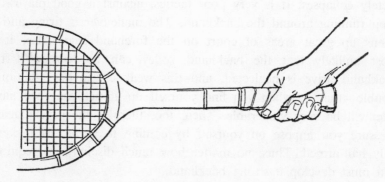

The Eastern backhand grip with thumb placed directly behind the racket handle (top).

The same grip seen from overhead (middle).

The Eastern backhand grip with thumb placed diagonally on the racket handle (bottom).

To assume the Eastern backhand grip, take the Eastern forehand grip, in which the palm is behind the handle, hold the racket in front of you, and move it one eighth of a turn to the right. This puts the palm of the hand on top of the handle and the thumb diagonally across the left side. The V formed by the thumb and forefinger lies on the upper left bevel of the handle. (The thumb can be placed along the length of the back of the handle if you feel that gives you better support.) The forefinger curls around the upper right bevel for better control.

Stroking the Backhand: As with the forehand, assume the ready position and watch the ball as it comes off your opponent's racket. Take the backhand grip and, as you move toward the ball, move the racket back with your left hand on the throat, turning your shoulders to the left. When you are close to the ball, place yourself in position for the stroke by putting your weight on the rear foot and bringing your right foot over toward the left sideline. When you are ready to make the stroke, your right foot should be two feet closer to the left sideline than your left foot, your right shoulder should be turned so that your back is almost to the net, and your weight should be mainly on your rear foot. Both knees should be bent, the right knee more than the left. As in hitting the forehand, if the ball is low, you must bend your knees lower to reach it. Do not try to scoop the ball up by lowering the racket head.

With the racket held parallel to the baseline and your right hand at about hip height, start the body turn to the right, releasing the racket with your left hand. The racket moves forward parallel to the ground, the body pivots forward and your weight is shifted onto your front foot. The racket is swung around, meets the ball with a perpendicular face about a foot in front of the right hip, and sweeps through, rising slightly in a long, smooth follow-through. At the end of the follow-through, your right arm should be fully extended; the racket should be well past the right shoulder and at about head height. Topspin is imparted naturally by the swing of the arm, the wrist tending to turn over as the racket is brought forward.

The backhand drive (front view)

The backhand drive (side view)

You must take great care to keep both your grip and wrist very firm on the backhand or you are likely to flub the shot.

The Backhand Chop: This is often called a backhand slice, but since it consists of a downward movement of the racket instead of a sideward one, chop is probably a more accurate designation.

Like the forehand chop, this should be considered a supplementary shot to the drive—a method of confusing your opponent with spin. It should not be used too often.

Assume the Continental grip, as for the forehand chop. Place your feet and body as you would for the backhand drive, but cock your wrist upward so that the racket head is about shoulder height. The hand holding the racket should be at waist height, while the left hand supports the throat, as for the drive.

The swing is downward, with the face of the racket being kept open (uptilted) by the upward-cocked position of the wrist. The wrist is kept cocked all through the stroke, causing the racket strings to hit the ball from underneath as they move forward, imparting backspin. The follow-through is slight, with the racket stopping when the head is near the right knee.

CHAPTER FIVE

The Serve

In today's tennis the serve is the most important single stroke. It is the one stroke that is not affected by the shot your opponent has made—the only one that gives you complete control over the way the ball will be hit.

Uses of the Serve: In the early days of the game, the serve was used merely to put the ball in play. It was hit into the proper court underhand and a player was considered unsporting if he hit the stroke overhand. But in 1912 an American player, Maurice Mc-Loughlin, showed what a powerful offensive weapon the serve could be and inspired later generations of players to make use of it as a primary attacking stroke. The motion of the serve is a lot like throwing, and because of their affinity for sports in which throwing plays a large part, Americans have always been noted for the strength of their services—Tilden, Vines, John Doeg, Jack Kramer, Arthur Ashe. One American, Bob Falkenburg, captured the Wimbledon title with his serve and volley and not much else. Since he was able to hold his serve consistently against the finest opposition, all he needed was a single breakthrough to win a set.

Psychologically, the serve should be regarded as a means of putting your opponent on the defensive, after which you can outmaneuver him and finally hit a placement or force him into an error.

Many beginning players, however, think of the first serve exclusively as a quick means of winning the point—that is, by an ace; and the second serve (should the first be a fault) merely as a means of putting the ball in play—the old-fashioned attitude. What usually happens is that the first serve, hit hard and flat, is a fault. The second serve—because it might go in to avoid a double-fault—is blooped high over the net and kept shallow so that it will not go beyond the back service line.

The player who throws his first serve away in this manner and hits a weak second serve puts himself at a great disadvantage. The receiver, after watching the first serve fail, can move in to attack, confident that the second serve will be easy to handle.

In addition to losing points, the server who uses this technique is tiring himself needlessly. He is serving nearly twice as many balls as he should and serving harder than he should. At the end of a couple of grueling sets he may wish he had conserved his strength.

It is important to get the first serve in at least 75 per cent of the time. A consistent, well-placed serve presents you with these two advantages: by serving to your opponent's weakness, you may win some points outright or force weak returns which can be hit deep to the corners; and by pulling your opponent out of the court with wide-hit serves, you create openings which can be exploited by groundstrokes. Occasionally you may hit an ACE—a serve that your opponent cannot get his racket on.

Of the three types of serves—THE SLICE, the FLAT SERVE (or CANNONBALL) and the AMERICAN TWIST—only the slice serve should be used by beginners. The flat serve is too hard to control to be counted on, and the American twist, which requires a pronounced bending of the back, extremely fine timing, and very strong control of the wrist, is used by only the most advanced players.

Hitting the Slice Serve: In contrast to the flat serve, the slice serve allows the server to hit a reasonably hard ball that is kept under control by the sideward spin. If practiced diligently, it will land consistently in the opponent's service courts. It can be hit without a great deal of effort and the spin imparted often gives the receiver trouble.

Because slice is to be imparted to the ball, you should not use the Eastern forehand grip, but the Continental—that is, a grip halfway between the Eastern forehand and Eastern backhand. This grip allows very free wrist action, which is undesirable in the groundstrokes, but useful for the serve. How to obtain it has been described in the section on the forehand chop.

In serving to the deuce court, place the toes of your left foot about an inch behind the baseline and as near as possible to its center. Your body should be sideways to the net, with your left foot at about a 45-degree angle to the baseline to make it easier for you to turn. Your right foot should be placed about eighteen inches from your left, parallel to the baseline and about six inches closer to the right sideline. Your weight should be evenly distributed on both feet.

The actions of the serve should be rhythmic, with both arms performing their functions simultaneously. Before you make the toss, place your feet in the proper position at the baseline and take the service grip. Hold the racket with the handle at waist height and the racket head opposite your left hip but about a foot away from it. The head of the racket should be slightly higher than the handle. The ball, held in the fingers of the left hand, should be placed against the racket strings. The right arm is relaxed and slightly bent, the left arm forms about a 90-degree angle. Weight now shifts to the rear foot. This position allows you to start the movements for the toss and the backswing at the same time.

As your left hand tosses the ball up, your right hand and arm should bring the racket back and up. At the completion of the toss, the left arm should be fully extended, while the right hand, with the right elbow sharply bent, should be quite near your right ear. The racket is held horizontally behind your head. When the ball reaches its highest point in the toss and begins its descent, your right arm and shoulder come forward and the arm is extended so that you can make full use of your reach. As the right arm moves forward, the left arm moves down, the body twisting to the left and your weight is transferred onto the forward foot. You should hit the ball about a foot inside the baseline and with the racket arm outstretched. As the ball is hit, the wrist moves forward and down, imparting extra SIDESPIN, or slice. The sidespin slows the speed of the ball somewhat, and helps keep it within the bounds of your opponent's service court.

After the ball is hit, bring the racket down and across your body, down past the left leg in smooth follow-through. Your right foot should come forward for balance and to allow you to get ready for your opponent's return.

The toss is an extremely important part of the serve and should be practiced by itself until you can place the ball where you can best hit it. The ball should be struck when it has reached the top of the toss and is just about to descend. A bad toss—one that is

The slice serve.

too high or too low or one too close to your body or too far in front of it—is apt to result in a bad serve.

In serving to the ad court, stand about three feet from the center of the baseline. This gives you a better angle for serving to your opponent's backhand and more opportunity to take returns on your forehand (presuming your forehand is the stronger side).

Place the toes of your left foot about an inch behind the baseline and place your right foot about six inches closer to the *left* sideline. Your feet should be about eighteen inches apart. The toss, backswing, forward swing, weight shift, point of impact, and follow-through are the same as for serving to the deuce court.

If your first serve goes out, you should quickly determine what went wrong and correct it. Perhaps your toss was not high enough or perhaps you did not put enough slice on the serve. (The more slice, the slower the ball will travel.) Most players put more slice on their second serve to make sure that it does not go beyond the rear service line. If your serve consistently goes out to the right or left, check your toss and if that is all right, change the position of your feet slightly. The ball usually goes in the direction the feet are pointing.

If your first serve goes into the net, perhaps you hit the ball too far in front of you—the result of a poor toss. Or perhaps you did not hit the ball in the center of your strings, losing some of the power of the racket. The next time you serve, make sure you look at the ball as your racket hits it.

Serving into the Sun: Occasionally, serving on a particular side of the court may give you trouble because the sun gets in your eyes. Wearing some kind of visor or dark glasses may alleviate this. Or you may find it advantageous to toss the ball a little farther to the right, allowing it to descend to a point slightly above head level and then hitting it, using plenty of slice. Because of the low trajectory, the ball should be hit fairly hard so that it will clear the net. It may also be advisable to stand nearer the sidelines when serving so that you will not have to look into the sun as you hit the ball.

Receiving the Serve: If the ability to serve is the most important element in tennis, the ability to return the serve is the second most important. If you cannot return the serve well, you will lose most of the games your opponent serves, and he will win his points without much of a struggle. This puts considerable pressure on you to win the majority of your own services, and the effort may be fatiguing. The pressure is, of course, self-imposed, and it can be avoided if you make it a practice to develop a good, steady service return—one that at least keeps the ball in play and may occasionally be used offensively.

If you can judge your opponent's best serves well and hit them back consistently, you will deal him a serious psychological blow.

A player who sees that his serves win points handily is going to concentrate hard, serve energetically, and try to take these points quickly; but if he finds that his trickiest serves come back and that careless serves are attacked, he is going to become very discouraged. He may try too hard to hit effective serves or he may be content merely to put the ball in play. In either case, what should be one of his best weapons has been blunted.

In receiving the serve in the deuce court, stand about a yard in front of the baseline and a yard to the left of the singles sideline. This gives you a chance to take most serves on your forehand but does not leave a huge gap on the left side of the service court. If you have a weak backhand that you want to protect and the server does not hit the ball hard, stand about two yards to the left of the right singles sideline.

Assume the ready position—weight on the balls of the feet, head up, knees slightly bent, racket held out in front of you and the throat supported by your left hand. Since you will be expecting to hit a forehand drive, you should hold the racket in the Eastern forehand grip, but do not grip the handle tightly, as this will make your entire arm tense and interfere with a smooth backswing. If you see that the serve must be taken on the backhand, change to the Eastern backhand grip as you start your pivot to the left.

In order to get a jump on the ball it is extremely important to watch the toss and the server's backswing. This will help you to sight the actual meeting of his racket with the ball. The moment you determine where the ball is headed—to your forehand or backhand or directly at you—move toward the best position from which to hit it and, while moving, get the racket back and turn the shoulders and body. Watch the flight of the ball carefully—speed, angle, and trajectory—and determine where it will land in the service box. Then place yourself accordingly. Watch the ball bounce, and hit it smoothly at about hip level, the way you would a forehand or backhand drive, the racket fully extended. Finish the stroke with a smooth follow-through.

To receive the serve in the the ad court, stand approximately on the left singles sideline, about a yard inside the baseline. Assume the ready position, taking the forehand grip as you would when

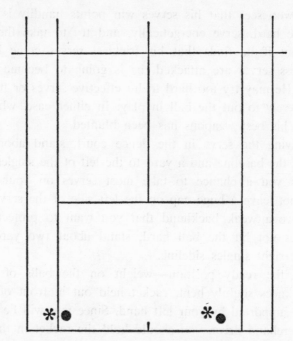

The proper positions for receiving the serve in the deuce and advantage courts. (The black circles show normal receiving positions. The black asterisks show positions to protect the backhand.)

receiving in the deuce court. Watch the ball closely from the time of the server's toss and move into position, bringing the racket back the moment you can ascertain the ball's direction. Get set to hit and stroke the ball at about hip level, following through smoothly and getting ready for the next shot.

As you progress in tennis, meeting stronger opponents, serves will probably begin coming in harder and deeper. In this case, you should stand approximately on the baseline.

If your opponent has a weak second serve and you have a good, dependable forehand, move in a step and get ready to take the ball on your forehand, hitting it deep to his backhand corner.

Sometimes you can tempt your opponent to serve where you want him to, merely by the expedient of leaving a hole in your court that is not too obvious but which he cannot refrain from aiming at. Thus, in the ad court, if you want to be sure of making him hit a serve to your forehand, play far to the left. He will see the space and he will be tempted to place the ball in it. You must be careful to move to cover it quickly, of course, or you may be the victim of an ace.

If you find you are not returning serves consistently, check these things: watching the ball from the time your opponent tosses it up; getting the racket back *early;* keeping a firm grip as you hit the ball; taking the ball away from your body so that your swing will not be cramped; concentrating hard as you follow the flight of the ball and stroke it.

If you are playing an opponent who has a very strong serve that you have trouble getting back, check all the things you might be doing wrong (particularly getting the racket back soon enough) and keep trying to return the ball. After a while you will adapt to the timing and your returns will start falling in.

CHAPTER SIX

The Volley

Volleying is hitting the ball before it bounces—generally in the area near the net—and in today's top-level tennis it is as important a shot as the groundstrokes. In doubles, it is considered even more important.

Some players—especially girls—find it difficult to volley and are therefore reluctant to take the net, where they must make use of this stroke. The volley is harder to hit than groundstrokes—it requires more wrist and hand strength and faster reflexes—but it is a shot that, if practiced faithfully, gets easier all the time. If you have confidence in the shot, you will volley well.

Uses of the Volley: Here are some advantages you will gain once you develop a consistent volley. If you hit a deep groundstroke and force a weak return, you can hit the return deep and come to net, where you may be able to volley your opponent's next shot out of his reach. If your opponent hits a relatively high, slow ball, you do not have to wait for it to bounce but can move forward, take it on the volley, and post yourself at the net—almost always an advantageous position. Also, hitting the ball before it bounces gives your opponent less time to get into position for his return. When you have accumulated experience, you may wish to follow your serve in to net; your next shot will generally be a volley. In doubles, when your partner serves you will play net, where you are expected to volley; and on some forcing shots (if you play

The Volley41

doubles correctly), both you and your partner will be playing net and volleying. Finally, if your opponent knows you are a good volleyer, he will have to hit shots that keep you from coming to the net, and because he must keep them deep, a great many of these shots may go out of court.

Hitting the Volley: There is no time to change grips while volleying, so you should use the Eastern backhand grip. This gives you a firm grip on the backhand side and, because of the way the stroke is made, it is equally effective for forehand volleys.

As you stand about six feet from the net, awaiting the ball, you should hold the racket straight out in front and tilted upward at a 45-degree angle. This way it can be moved to the left or right with equal facility. The racket head should be kept higher than the wrist at all times—while stroking and in the ready position.

While waiting for the ball, you should have your weight on the balls of your feet and be ready to move to either side the moment your opponent hits the ball. It is essential to watch the ball as his racket meets it and to follow it carefully as it comes off the strings. This will enable you to determine where the ball is going the instant your opponent hits it. In time, your instinct to react quickly will give you confidence in your ability to hit the most difficult volleys.

The volley is not stroked but *punched.* It can be compared to a boxer's jab, as opposed to a roundhouse swing. The fact that you hit the ball before it bounces and move forward as you hit it affords you all the speed you need; a long backswing is not necessary—nor is there time to make it. The short jab swing allows more control over your racket and permits less chance for error.

If the ball comes to you on the forehand side and is some distance away, quickly bring the racket back, turn your shoulders and pivot your body to the right, moving your left foot over toward the right sideline and placing it as close to the sideline as your right foot. The racket and arm should make about a 45-degree angle to the baseline when the backswing is completed. Your knees should be slightly bent. If the ball is close, merely turn your shoulders.

Watching the ball carefully, grip the racket handle firmly, bring the racket forward with a crisp movement and, keeping a very firm wrist, hit the ball when it is about two feet in front of you. As the racket comes forward, shift your weight forward, leaning into the shot. The margin of error on some volleyed shots is so small that great care must be taken to watch the ball until you actually see the racket strings meet it.

If you see that you must volley the ball below the level of the net, get down to it by bending your knees—not by lowering the racket head. Your wrist should never be higher than the racket head or you will find yourself misjudging the ball. If the shot is taken low, the racket face should be slightly uptilted so that the ball will not go into the net.

In volleying on the backhand side, assume the ready position and, watching the ball closely, bring the racket back, turn your

The forehand volley:

shoulders and pivot to the left. For wide shots, your right foot should move quickly to the left, to a point about six inches closer to the left sideline than your left foot. Your right knee should be bent. Your wrist should be cocked and your grip should be very firm.

You should hit the ball when it is about two feet in front of your body, bringing the racket forward firmly, meeting the ball solidly and leaning into the shot. If the ball is below the level of the net, bend the knees sharply to get down to it. Make sure that the handle is lower than the head of the racket as you meet the ball.

For both forehand and backhand, because of the jabbing nature of the shot, there is only a slight follow-through. After making the volley, you should immediately assume the ready position for your opponent's possible return.

If your opponent's shot comes directly at you, it is best to take the ball with the backhand, as you would a shot coming toward the body in table tennis. The body turns slightly to the left, the left foot is moved backward and to the right, allowing an easy

Note "punching" motion of the shot.

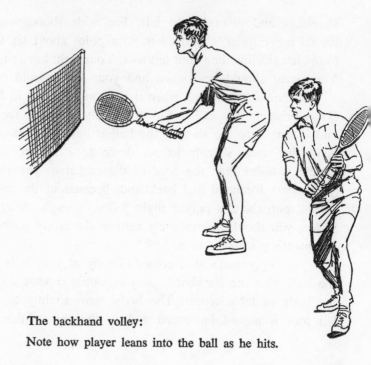

The backhand volley:

Note how player leans into the ball as he hits.

pivot, and the racket is brought quickly back. The ball should be watched very closely and struck about a foot in front of the body. As with the other volleys, you should try to lean into the ball as you bring the racket forward.

If a ball comes quite wide on either the backhand or forehand while you are at net, you may have to take a very long step with the moving foot and reach far to the side with the racket, cutting down on your backswing; or you may have to take several steps. In either case, the grip should be very firm, the line of the shoulders should be at almost right angles to the net and you should try to move forward into the shot as you hit it.

In matches, one thing the volleyer must watch out for is the lob. He must not only be ready to move quickly to the left or right but also to retreat, meanwhile preparing for a smash.

As you develop your volley, try to get to the ball more and more quickly. The sooner you can reach it, the more pressure you will put on your opponent. Also, the sooner you take it, the more opportunity you will have to hit down on the ball—as opposed to hitting it horizontally or upward—and thus the harder you can hit it with a good margin of safety.

The Half-Volley: This is an emergency shot which should be avoided by all beginning players, since it requires extremely delicate timing and fine touch. On a HALF-VOLLEY the ball is hit almost immediately after it bounces—at a height of about eight inches from the ground. The action of the racket meeting the ball is something like the dropkick in football.

Few players *want* to hit a half-volley, but they do it out of necessity—usually when they are advancing to the net and must hit a ball that lands too far in front of them to volley but too far back to hit with a groundstroke. Or an opponent may hit a

The forehand half-volley

The backhand half-volley

Note how player gets down to the ball by bending his knees.

Again note how player bends his knees in an effort to keep the racket head higher than the handle.

hard shot when a player is trapped in the vicinity of the rear service line. In both cases, the player must thrust the head of his racket down, crouching to the ball if he has time, and block it as it comes rapidly up off the court. There are many chances for errors and there is very little chance of placing the ball accurately. It is useful to know what a half-volley is, but only the experts handle the shot well enough to make use of it as part of their game.

CHAPTER SEVEN

The Lob

A good, dependable lob—a stroke in which the racket comes up and under the ball, sending it high in the air—should be in every player's repertory. The shot will save dozens of points in a set and, against some opponents, may even turn the tide when all seems lost.

These are the principal uses of the lob:

(1) Returning a deep, wide-angled shot, giving yourself time to get back to the center of the court to await the next offering.

(2) Driving a persistent net player back and forcing him to play farther from the net than he would like to. (The farther back the net player stands, the more difficult it is to volley accurately.)

(3) Changing the pace of the game when your opponent has no trouble in returning conventional drives. Some players find a hard, low shot easier to return than a slow, tantalizing one. A steady diet of this type of shot may tempt your opponent to try for winners, and he may not have the strokes to hit them.

(4) As an offensive weapon after you have drawn a player in close with a drop shot. Chasing lobs repeatedly from the front of the court to the back can be very tiring.

(5) Defending against an aggressive smasher. In most cases a good smasher will win points if he gets the chance to use this shot, but accurate, steady, lobbed returns of his smashes are very useful

The forehand flat l◦

for two reasons: hitting repeated overheads can be quite tiring, and fatigue may make itself felt toward the end of the match; and, second, if the lobs keep coming back, the smasher may become impatient or discouraged, lose concentration, and miss.

(6) In doubles, the lob is especially useful to give you or your partner time to return to the court after being drawn wide, to drive net players back from the net and as a service return that may give the serving team trouble.

There are, however, dangers in making too much use of the lob. Some are tactical and one is psychological.

The stroke should not be used too often as a counter to net-rushing or your opponent will begin to expect it. He will stay back a little, or prepare to move backward after going forward, then take his time and hit a confident smash. The lob should be varied with drives hit crosscourt or down the sidelines or directly at the net-rusher. Of course, if your opponent's approach shots are so deep and hard that they cannot be returned accurately, it is better to lob—taking a chance on his failing to put the ball away—than to hit out or into the net or giving him an easy volley.

The lob must be hit very carefully to make sure that it goes where it is intended—that is, high enough to pass over the head

of the net player and deep in your opponent's court—but inside the baseline. If a lob is too low or falls short, it presents an easy target to your opponent and he will probably win the point.

You may find that using the lob is very successful against your opponents as a point winner—they may miss smashes or misjudge their drives. However, it should not be used so much that you neglect the development of other strokes—the drives, volley, and smash. A player who lobs a great deal is defense-minded and, in the most advanced stages of tennis, the best players are the hard-hitting, aggressive ones.

Hitting the Lob: There are three kinds of lobs—the flat lob, the sliced lob, and the topspin lob. The last-named shot is rarely used, even among the very best players, because it is so difficult to control. Basically, topspin is imparted by a fast upward movement of the wrist as the racket is brought toward the ball. The spin causes the ball to drop rapidly after it has reached the top of its trajectory and, after it bounces, to skitter quickly toward the fence behind the court, making it very hard to catch up with. Chuck McKinley, the former American and Wimbledon champion, is its most notable exponent, but since it is so difficult and risky a shot it is not recommended for beginning players.

The footwork for hitting both the flat lob and the sliced lob is the same as for the groundstrokes. On the forehand, the front foot is about six inches closer to the right sideline than the rear foot; on the backhand, the front foot is about a foot closer to the left sideline than the rear foot. For both backhand and forehand, as the racket is drawn back, weight is on the rear foot.

For the flat lob, which beginners should learn first, the Eastern forehand grip is used on the forehand and the Eastern backhand grip on the backhand. When hitting a forehand lob, the racket is drawn back and held a little bit lower than on the forehand drive, and to make sure the racket gets under the ball, the left knee is more sharply bent. As the ball descends after bouncing, the racket is brought forward under it with the face slightly tilted upward. The upward tilting of the racket face and the upward movement of the arm impart lift to the ball, ending it on an upward arc. The forward swing should be gentle and highly controlled, and the wrist and grip should be kept quite firm throughout the swing. The ball should be watched closely all through the stroke. At its completion the racket should be about head high, and your weight should be on your left foot.

In hitting the flat lob on the backhand side, the racket should be drawn far back in plenty of time and the forward knee should be quite sharply bent to allow the racket head, with its face slightly tilted, to get under the ball. The stroke is made upward, with the wrist very firm, and at the end of the follow-through the racket should be at about head height.

The backhand flat lob.

In the sliced lob, the racket is not swung so much under the ball and upward as it is for the flat lob. It is brought forward in a more nearly horizontal manner, although its face is tilted upward, and it comes forward faster. Instead of hitting the ball flat and somewhat gently, the strings bite into the ball from underneath, imparting backspin. The speed of the racket, combined with its upward tilt and the cutting motion of the strings, sends the ball high in the air. Because of the backspin, the ball can go higher than the flat lob and still stay within the court.

The flat lob is easier to master than the sliced lob because the racket, held low, is brought upward and follows the direct path of the ball. This lob is solidly hit, whereas for the sliced lob the racket moves in an almost horizontal path and the strings cut across the ball, imparting UNDERSPIN. The ball is thrust into the air by the horizontal movement of the racket and the angle of the racket face. The timing is relatively difficult to master without a good deal of practice.

If you should try to master the sliced lob, you may find the Continental grip more effective than the Eastern forehand and back-hand grips, since the former allows the racket head to be tilted back with less effort.

The best place to aim a lob is over the left shoulder of the man at net. In order to smash a ball thus hit the net man must quickly move back and to his left while somehow managing to raise his racket high above his left ear. His alternative is to smash with his backhand, a very difficult shot.

When you are placed completely on the defensive and all you wish to do is return the ball safely so that you can scurry back to the center of the court, the safest lob is usually one that is hit crosscourt. This gives you several extra feet in which to place the ball and causes your opponent to do a little extra running.

The lob is the stroke most affected by the wind, so take careful note of the wind direction and strength if you intend to hit a number of lobs or if you are playing someone who may force you to lob. When the wind is behind your back you should seldom lob, since the ball may be blown beyond the baseline. In this case, if you volley well, you should go to the net a good deal because your opponent's attempted passing shots will be slowed down. Against the wind, lobs are useful defensive strokes, especially high lobs that your opponent may have difficulty judging. The backspin on a sliced lob, if you hit this stroke well, controls the ball better against the wind than does the slight amount of spin on a flat-hit lob.

CHAPTER EIGHT

The Smash

The smash is the most spectacular shot in tennis and it is one of the most satisfying shots to hit. It consists of bringing the racket down rapidly and forcefully on a high ball—generally a lob—and slamming it into your opponent's court. If the shot is hit properly from the front part of the court, its speed should force your opponent to make an error if he can reach the ball at all.

In essence, the stroke can be thought of as a serve for which your opponent has obligingly tossed up the ball. However, the ball is hit from a point close to the net and you have the entire court in which to place it, so the shot is many times more devastating than the most severe serve.

Uses of the Smash: The smash is one of your major weapons, along with the volley, if you wish to play aggressive tennis. If you have a good smash and can score with it consistently, your effectiveness at net will be greatly increased, because your opponent, fearing your smash, may start hitting lobs outside the court or send drives into the net in an attempt to pass you.

You get a nice psychological lift, too, from successful smashes. After putting your opponent on the defensive and making him hit the ball in the air, you line up his shot and slam it where he cannot return it—a most rewarding experience.

Hitting the Smash: As you see a lob come off your opponent's racket, you should prepare for the smash by taking the proper grip —the Continental grip, also used for the service—and moving into position. Whether you let the ball bounce and then hit it, or take it on the fly, your position should be one that allows you to hit the ball with the upraised racket and outstretched arm at a point nearly over your right shoulder but about a foot in front of it. Your body should be at right angles to the net, right foot advanced and your weight on the rear foot.

Getting into position *early* is the most important part of smashing because it is easy to misjudge the precise point where the ball will drop in relation to your forward swing. You must allow yourself time to make slight adjustments of your feet to be sure that you will not hit the ball too far in front of you or too far in back. Hitting the ball too far in front of the body will cause it to go into the net; hitting it too far in back will cause it to go beyond the baseline. There is also the problem of hitting too late or too early, which can also cause errors. By getting ready in plenty of time— feet positioned, body turned, racket back, balance steady—you can concentrate on the nearly vertical flight of the ball.

You should avoid a long, downward sweep for your backswing, since this merely delays getting the racket ready. Bring the racket up in front—it will save time. After you have established your approximate position under the ball while it is still high in the air, raise the racket behind your head, cocking your right arm. The racket is held in place, with the strings a little above head level. For the sake of balance, the left arm is held forward, and above the head, nearly fully extended, and can be used as a kind of sighting device as the ball descends. While the racket is back in this position you should make your final judgments as to the precise placing of your feet. When the ball descends into the hitting area, you quickly bring the racket forward and as the racket, arm, and right shoulder come forward, your weight is transferred from the rear foot to the front. The ball is hit flat and the racket is brought down across the body from right to left in a smooth follow-through. At the finish of the smash, the racket head swings down past the left knee.

While you should straighten your arm as you hit the ball so that the racket is as high over your head as possible, additional power can be put into the smash (as with the service) if you snap your wrist forward, bringing the racket down over the ball and, in a sense, covering it with the strings.

Since it is easier to smash a ball after it has bounced, beginning players should smash this kind of shot first. In hitting smashes after the ball has bounced, you must remember that your position will be much farther back in the court that when you smash *before* the ball bounces, and since you are farther back in the court, you cannot hit the ball at as steep an angle because it will go into the net.

Once you have mastered hitting smashes after the ball has bounced, you should start hitting them at points closer to the net— taking the ball *before* it bounces. When you have developed confidence in the stroke, you should think of it as a means of ending the point. You do not have to aim close to the lines, since the ball will be traveling rapidly off your racket, but you should hit it in the direction of the corners, especially the backhand corner. It is foolish to aim for a line and lose the point by having the smash go out.

The smash.

One common mistake even experienced smashers make is to become overconfident. Sometimes lobs float over the net looking so vulnerable that the smasher refuses to move the few inches that would enable him to make a winning shot, or he becomes over-eager at the prospect of killing a SETUP and hits too early. As a result, he fluffs the shot. The cure for this is to prepare in plenty of time, even for the easiest-looking shot, and treat it with the same care you would a very difficult one.

Smashing into the Sun: Often the net player will find himself smashing into the sun, since the lobbing player knows how difficult this can be and figures to win a few points by the stratagem. There are several solutions to the problem. One is wearing a visor,

a long-brimmed cap, or an Australian hat. Dark glasses are also useful. On some lobs it may be advisable to let the ball bounce, then position yourself to hit it from a point where the sun does not strike your eyes as you meet the ball. Or, after letting the ball bounce, you can hit it with a drive to one corner or the other. Still another way to solve the problem is to let the ball bounce and then hit it at about head level with a slice, much like the slice service.

The Backhand Smash: Occasionally you will be put in the position of having to hit a smash from your backhand side. Unless you have anticipated it, a well-placed lob, aimed high over your left shoulder by a shrewd opponent, cannot be volleyed or smashed on the forehand side. In this case, you should turn quickly to the left, chase the ball and stretch out your arm and racket to reach it. With your back to the net, hit the ball in a downward motion and, for extra speed—since you cannot get your body behind the shot—snap your wrist, adding impetus to the stroke. In the follow-through, bring the racket down to the right side of your body.

This is one of the most difficult shots in tennis, requiring fine timing and excellent wrist control. If your opponent repeatedly forces you to make this shot by lobbing over your left shoulder, play farther to the left while at net or move quickly to that side when you see he is going to lob. Almost all smashes can be taken on the forehand side if you anticipate well and if you move into position quickly.

CHAPTER NINE

The Drop Shot

The drop shot is a very delicately hit touch shot, the purpose of which is to take most of the speed off your opponent's ball and send it back into his court as close to the net as possible. It should be hit with a good deal of backspin, the racket being brought down on the ball in a short chopping motion. The backspin causes the ball to bounce nearly straight up and down, requiring your opponent to extend his arm to its fullest or to take an extra step when he runs in to retrieve it.

While the shot is quite effective against players who are not too alert, or who move slowly about the court, or who do not hit hard, it is usually ineffective against a hard hitter. A hard-hit ball does not allow the drop-shot artist the time he needs to draw the racket across the ball with the required finesse. Hit off a fast-moving ball, the drop shot may land closer to the service line than to the net, allowing an opponent to swoop in on the ball, direct it to one corner or another, and establish himself in the forecourt. Against an alert player and one who moves fast, the drop-shot specialist may find himself hitting many shots into the net because he must place the ball extremely close to it in order to keep his opponent from replying with a devastating counter.

These are the occasions when the drop shot is most valuable:

(1) When your opponent shows a reluctance to come to the net. The drop shot brings him forward and may make him vulnerable after he retrieves the ball.

(2) When your opponent is tired or slow. The drop shot makes use of the length of the court to make him run, and if he retrieves the ball he can be made to scurry back to the baseline for a lob. If the sequence is repeated often, your opponent may become quite fatigued.

(3) As a weapon of surprise. Occasionally the drop shot on return of service is effective if the server likes to stay back at the baseline—especially on the second, and usually slower, serve.

(4) On a court with a slow surface—such as slightly moist clay, where the shot will take an especially low bounce.

(5) Though it may not be chivalrous to mention it—against girls. It has been shown over and over again that girl players are much more willing to run from side to side than they are up and back. Perhaps this stems from their reluctance to come to net, or perhaps they do not feel comfortable making an extra effort to retrieve the shot. In any event, one of the most glaring weaknesses of most girl players is their inability to return drop shots. In mixed doubles, many points can be won from a girl server by hitting crosscourt drop shots, with the receiving team moving in to cut off the return. The shot is also effective in rallies, if the girl player shows a tendency to hang back at the baseline.

Among the top players, one sees the shot used much more often in ladies' singles than in men's. Of the top lady players, Maria Bueno is probably its most effective practitioner.

The answer to the drop shot is either another drop shot (if your opponent hangs back), a lob (if he is close to the net), or a ball hit hard to an open spot on the court. When you hit a drop shot, you must never assume that you have won the point and can relax. If your opponent is alert and fast, or if the shot goes too high or too deep, the fact that he is hitting the ball from a point close to the net means that he has a choice of several places to put the ball, and you do not have much time to reach it for your return. You must be ready to run forward or to either side to get your opponent's shot, no matter how difficult it looks for him to make it.

You should never hit a drop shot from the back of the court because it is so difficult to place accurately and because your opponent has plenty of time to see the ball coming and move in for it. Nor should you drop shot against a player who likes to play net. He is looking for a shot he can come in on and the drop shot supplies it. Finally, the shot is generally ineffective in the wind, because it is so hard to place accurately, and on courts like cement and hard clay where the bounce is relatively high.

Hitting the Drop Shot: The backswing motion and the footwork are the same as those for the backhand and forehand drive. However, the forward motion of the arm and body are slower. Near the moment of impact the racket face should be slightly open and the ball should be struck with a downward rather than a straight-through movement of the arm. Because you are trying to take speed off your opponent's ball, the follow-through is minimized. It is extremely important to watch the ball as it is being struck, since

The forehand drop shot.

the shot requires very fine timing. For crosscourt shots, the ball should be hit well in front of the body. For a drop shot aimed DOWN THE LINE, the ball should be taken later on both forehand and backhand.

The crosscourt drop shot is the one most frequently used because the ball travels somewhat laterally as it goes toward your opponent's court and you do not run as much risk of hitting it deep; there is much less margin for error in the down-the-line drop shot.

As far as the grip is concerned, you may find that you have better control of the shot with the Continental grip—a natural grip

The backhand drop sh

for the soft, delicate chopping motion used for the drop shot. This grip may be used for both forehand and backhand drop shots.

The Dink: A shot akin to the drop shot is the DINK. This is used primarily in advanced doubles as a return of service. The ball is hit softly crosscourt and clears the net by a slight margin. Its purpose is to force the inrushing server to hit the ball up—allowing the receiving team to hit down on it and take the offensive. The shot requires so much touch and control, however, that beginning players are not advised to make use of it.

CHAPTER TEN

Spin

A working knowledge of spin—how it can be used, how to apply it and how to cope with it—is very useful to the tennis player.

There are four basic types of spin, something akin to the four points of the compass:

(1) Topspin (sometimes called OVERSPIN) is used on the groundstrokes, both forehand and backhand.

(2) Backspin (sometimes called underspin) is used on the chop and the drop shot.

(3) Sidespin from right to left is used by some players on a forehand shot called a slice.

(4) Sidespin from left to right is used on some low backhands, on the slice serve, and occasionally on forehand smashes.

(A fifth type of spin, used for the American twist serve, is a combination of topspin and sidespin. It is very difficult to apply and to control and will not be discussed here.)

How Spin Works: Here is why spin affects the flight of the ball: as the ball moves through the air, its fluffy surface meets with air resistance. If the ball is hit flat, it carries only a small amount of spin, and air resistance is theoretically equal over its entire surface, gravity being the only natural force affecting its flight. However, when it is spinning rapidly, one part of the ball meets the air with greater speed than the other parts. This causes more resistance to be built up against the part of the ball that moves the most

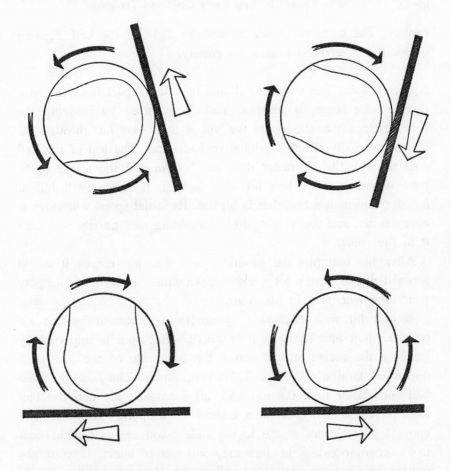

Topspin (seen from the side): Imparted by the racket strings coming up over the ball (white arrow)—as in forehand drive. The ball will sink after crossing the net and take a relatively long bounce (upper left).
Note: This represents the racket toward the *end* of the swing, when topspin is finally imparted.

Backspin (seen from the side): Imparted by a downward, somewhat slashing movement of the racket—as in the forehand chop and drop shot. The ball will rise because of the spin, then drop and take a short, somewhat vertical bounce (upper right).

Forehand sidespin (seen from overhead): The racket is brought sideways from right to left, as for the forehand slice. The ball spins rapidly from right to left and on landing will bounce to the right (lower left).

Backhand sidespin (seen from overhead): The racket is brought sideways from left to right, as for the backhand slice. The ball spins rapidly from left to right and on landing will bounce to the left. This is also the spin applied to the slice serve, the ball being struck at about four o'clock (lower right).

rapidly. The extra resistance affects the flight of the ball, fighting or sometimes giving an assist to gravity.

Applying Spin: The most useful spin in tennis, apart from the slice on the slice serve, is topspin. This is imparted by bringing the racket strings over the top of the ball as the racket hits through the ball on a solidly struck forehand or backhand. The top of the ball goes through the air faster than the bottom and the air tends to push down on it. A ball hit with topspin, therefore, will fall at a faster rate than a ball that is hit flat. Its initial speed will carry it over the net, and the weight of air combining with gravity will keep it in the court.

After the ball hits the ground, since the spin causes it to go forward, it will have a long, low bounce which is useful for keeping your opponent deep in his court.

A ball hit with backspin, by contrast, is carried by the air underneath it and tends to fight gravity. Backspin is imparted by bringing the racket strings across the underside of the ball in a downward motion. This is called a chop stroke. The bottom of the ball goes faster than the top and, after crossing the net, the ball sails on for a short distance instead of dropping abruptly. The chop is a dangerous stroke to use unless you have excellent control over it, because the ball may sail out of court. If your opponent is playing net, it is additionally dangerous because the ball hangs up long enough for him to hit down on it as it crosses the net. After landing in your opponent's court, the ball with backspin tends to bounce somewhat vertically. Therefore your opponent must move forward a step to hit it—a fact which bothers some players until they get accustomed to the shot.

Sidespin is imparted on the forehand by drawing the racket strings across the ball from right to left. The ball develops a sidewise spin which causes it to curve to the right—like a right-handed pitcher's incurve or screwball—and to bounce to the right (as you look at it) when it lands. In hitting a low forehand, a player might apply sidespin, but it is a relatively rare shot and not as effective as a flat-hit or topped drive.

On the backhand, sidespin is applied from left to right, usually on very low backhands sent from the middle or right-hand side of the court to the left—notably in the deuce-court service return in doubles. This is not a frequently used shot, either, and a flat-hit or topped backhand is preferable. The sidespin makes the ball bounce to your opponent's right when it lands. A forehand smash hit with severe sidespin also causes the ball to bounce to your opponent's right.

Sidespin is also applied to the slice service, making the ball curve from right to left—like a right-handed pitcher's outcurve—and bounce to your opponent's right when it lands.

How to Deal with Spin: In handling your opponent's spin, it is important to notice how he hits the ball. If he comes down on it with his racket, he is hitting a chop and the bounce will be nearly vertical. In this case you should plan to take the ball closer to the point where it bounces than you would a ball hit with topspin. If your opponent comes up over the ball, he is imparting topspin. The ball will come up off the court fast and the bounce will be long. You must prepare to swing quickly and you should stand farther back than you would to take a chopped ball. If you see pronounced sidespin imparted on the forehand, the ball will bounce away from you on your backhand side and in toward you on your forehand; if you see pronounced sidespin imparted on the backhand, the ball will bounce toward you on your backhand and away from you on your forehand.

In hitting a ball that has been given pronounced spin, you must take special pains to meet it solidly with the center of your racket and stroke through the shot firmly—otherwise the spin will partly guide the ball on its subsequent flight. By hitting solidly, with a firm grip and wrist, you are in a sense overpowering the spin with the force of your shot.

If you are playing net and a chopped ball is hit toward you, you should aim your volley little higher than you would for a ball hit flat, because the ball with backspin has a tendency to spin down off the racket. A chopped shot is often volleyed into the net if the volleyer is not careful. By the same token, a topped drive should be volleyed on a relatively horizontal plane, because the spin of the ball tends to make it pop upward off the volleyer's racket. Balls hit with sidespin present no special problem to the volleyer.

CHAPTER ELEVEN

Singles Tactics

The thing that makes tennis the most fun, once you have learned to return the ball steadily and place it approximately where you want to, is putting to use your knowledge of tactics. A good deal of time and effort must be spent in developing the various strokes; the reward comes when you apply them to outmaneuver an opponent.

Tennis is a kind of athletic chess. There is the opening gambit, the probing for a weakness, the attack and the defense. As in chess, what you do in a tennis match depends a great deal on what your opponent does. When he attacks in a certain area, you must either defend extremely well or mount your own attack. Occasionally his aggressive moves may leave him open to a counterattack. On the other hand, while you are on the attack you must never underestimate the defense he can array against you. And, as in chess, you must not get discouraged if his defense seems impenetrable; eventually you may find a vulnerable spot.

Tactics, the cerebral part of tennis, can be considered the most efficient way to give your opponent the shot he least likes to hit and to make use of your own best shots to give you control of the court. It can be divided into three major parts: general rules which have been proven to be sound over the years; ways to attack the weaknesses of your opponents; and emergency tactics—methods you employ when your opponent shows unexpected strength.

General Tactics: (1) Keep the ball in play. Even among the top players, more points are lost by making errors than by missing an opponent's placements. If you are patient, keep the ball deep and concentrate on every shot, your opponent is going to pile up errors.

(2) After every shot, even if you think you have hit a sure winner, return to the center of the court and get ready for your opponent's possible return. Assuming you have won the point ahead of time is a dangerous practice.

(3) If you have confidence in your groundstrokes and your opponent returns a short ball, hit deep to the backhand corner and come to the net.

(4) Mix up your shots. Hit forehands and backhands down the line and crosscourt. Don't rely too heavily on one shot, such as the drop shot or lob, or your opponent will soon anticipate you.

(5) Make sure of the easy shots—don't miss them through over-confidence. It is said of the great players that what distinguishes them is that they never miss the easy shots.

(6) If you *do* miss an easy shot, or several easy shots, don't let your opponent see that you are upset; this will give him renewed vigor and confidence.

(7) If your opponent plays a lot of net, try to keep him back with deep shots; when he is at net, lob over his head.

(8) In serving, try to get the first ball in, even at the sacrifice of some speed, and try to keep it deep.

Attacking Weaknesses: You should be able to determine, from watching your opponent play, or from exchanging strokes with him, whether or not he has any marked weaknesses. There are any number you might uncover: a weak backhand, a poor net game, a weak second serve, slowness in moving around the court, and so on. The combination of making use of your best shots and forcing your opponent to rely on his weakest ones should win you a great many points.

(1) If your opponent's backhand is weak, there are three ways to attack it: keep hitting shots to it until he makes an error; hit wide to his forehand and then hit wide to his backhand so that

he will have to make his shot on the run; put pressure on his backhand by hitting a ball deep to his backhand side and coming to the net.

(2) If your opponent's forehand is weak, apply the same tactics to attack the forehand.

(3) If your opponent is reluctant to come to the net, draw him close with short shots and then lob over his head or try to pass him with a shot down the line or crosscourt.

(4) If your opponent's groundstrokes consistently fall short, play in closer to the service line and direct your shots to the corners, making him run. If you volley well, follow these drives to the net.

(5) If you see that your opponent lacks confidence in his passing shots when you are at net and invariably lobs, get ready to move back for the lobs and smash them out of his reach. Even if you do not put them away, you will tire him because he has so much court to cover so quickly.

(6) If your opponent's serve—particularly his second serve—is weak, move in as he hits it and try to return it to the corners. If he sees you are making points through attacking it, he will have to hit it harder and may make some double-faults.

(7) If you see that your opponent is slow-moving or not in top condition, try to run him around the court. To do this, aim shots from corner to corner, advancing to hit from a point midway between the baseline and the rear service line if his returns are weak. If he plays back in the court, vary these tactics with drop shots, followed by a lob over his head or drives to the corners.

Emergency Tactics: These tactics are to be used when your opponent shows special strength in one particular area, or perhaps in several areas. You are losing and you must (*a*) ascertain why he is beating you and (*b*) what you can quickly do about it. What follows is a list of strong shots your opponent may have and the ways in which you can neutralize them.

(1) If he is extremely steady, returning everything that you hit until you finally miss: the best solution is to go to the net, even if your net game is not particularly strong. One reason that your opponent may be so steady is that he has the entire court in which

to make his returns. If you cut off some of this area by taking the net, he may feel the pressure and begin to miss. As the game continues, your play at net is bound to get better. You will feel more at home there and your reflexes and timing will improve. And even if you don't beat him, you will be getting great practice.

(2) If he has a very strong forehand that he hits fast and deep, forcing you to make weak returns: try to hit the ball to his backhand as often as possible. To do this, hit wide to his forehand, making him take the shot on the run, then hit to his backhand. If you try to hit to his backhand without first hitting to his forehand, he will merely play over farther to his left and you may start hitting balls wide of his left sideline. You might also try hitting balls short to his backhand; these he will have to take on that side.

(3) If he has a strong backhand: reverse the process just described, hitting wide to his forehand, then hitting to his forehand and drawing him up with short shots to his forehand.

(4) If he has a very strong serve: watch him closely as he makes his toss and brings his racket up and down onto the ball. If you concentrate, you can determine at a very early point where the ball is headed. The moment you see where it is going, bring your racket back and get your feet into position. You do not have to swing hard at the ball; merely meet it with the racket. Do not try anything fancy; just get the ball back into his court. Toward the end of the set or the match you may find that his serve is easier to handle because you have grown accustomed to its speed or because he has become fatigued. In the meantime, you should try hard to win your own serves, even if you have to expend a lot of energy to do it.

(5) If your opponent runs up to net whenever he gets a chance and wins points with his volleys: try to keep him back by hitting deep. If you find his smash is weak, try lobs when he is at net, especially lobs he must take on his backhand side. In trying to pass him, hit shots wide to his right and left and at him to see if he has any discernible volleying weakness. (Some players have trouble volleying balls hit directly at them.) After you have hit the attempted passing shot, be alert to retrieve his volley. If he has

made a poor volley, you may be able to hit your return past him or over his head for the point. Another solution would be to take the net yourself. His groundstrokes may not be as good as his volleying, and finding you at net may disconcert him. In any event, while *you* are up there, *he* cannot be there.

(6) If he hits all kinds of tricky cuts and slices that take strange bounces: the first time you encounter them, these shots can be quite upsetting. Little by little, however, you will become accustomed to their spins and bounces and will be able to return them accurately. Watch the ball as it comes off your opponent's racket and follow its flight closely. Get ready for the shot in plenty of time, watch the ball as your racket meets it, and hit it solidly. If you have confidence in your volley, you should take the net at every opportunity; in volleying, you do not have to worry about the bounce your opponent's ball will take. Also, volleying these types of shots is easier than volleying drives because they travel more slowly and do not dip after crossing the net. Cut and chopped shots are ideal for the player who likes to move forward and hit the ball before it bounces.

Court Surfaces: It might be useful to say something here about court surfaces, since the kind of bounce the ball takes will affect the tactics you employ.

(1) On a relatively slow surface, such as clay, the ball bounces fairly high and you usually have enough time to get to it. Retrievers —players who have a steady, if unspectacular game—do well on a clay surface, while power hitters may be at a slight disadvantage. Often the winning player is the one who plays conservative, patient tennis.

(2) On relatively fast surfaces, like grass, cement, and wood, the power player has an advantage. The ball bounces low and long, sometimes skidding, and it is often difficult to get your racket back in time to make an effective drive. The retriever will find himself ineffective against an accurate hard-hitter; balls that he hits short will be slammed to the corners and his opponent will present a formidable threat at the net. Rallies are generally of shorter duration on these types of surfaces.

(3) Occasionally you may find yourself playing on a court that is in bad condition—the surface has holes or bumps that make the bounce of the ball inconsistent and difficult to judge. In this case, you should take the net at every opportunity—even if you are not quite at home there—because in so doing you will be able to hit the ball *before* it bounces.

Tactics for Girl Players: Most girls do not hit as hard, have the variety of strokes, or move around the court as fast as male players, and therefore they are somewhat limited as to the tactics they can employ.

Girls' strengths are usually the forehand, which they can place well, and the lob, which they can hit deep consistently. They are likely to be more patient than male players in trying to win a point and they may play more steadily. They are relatively weak, however, in such strokes as the serve, the backhand, the volley, and the smash. They run well from side to side on the court, but are not fast in running up and back.

It would be extremely useful for you, the girl player, to develop a dependable drop shot to supplement your basic strokes. It opens up a whole new field of tactics for girls' tennis. If you have a good drop shot, you can make use of this combination of shots: a deep forehand drive down the line; a soft drop shot hit crosscourt to your opponent's forehand, near the net; a lob into her backhand corner. You can see how much fast running this series of shots makes your opponent do—from the baseline to the net, diagonally, and back to the baseline diagonally. And here she must hit one of the most difficult shots for right-handers that has ever been thought up—a high-bouncing backhand from the back of the court.

This is another combination you might use: hit a crosscourt drive deep to the forehand; move in, hitting the return very delicately to the backhand close to the net; then either lob to the backhand corner or hit another drive deep to the forehand corner. The drop shot is also useful to draw your opponent in if she does not like the vicinity of the net or as a surprise crosscourt service return.

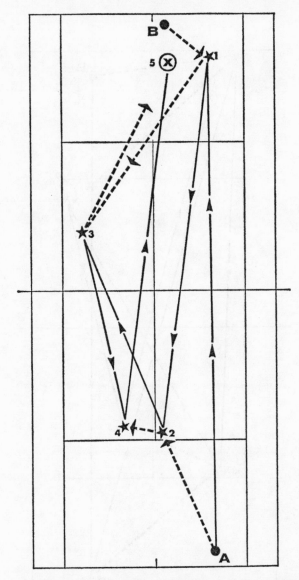

A sequence of shots that can be used by a girl player to win a point while tiring her opponent: Player A (the attacker) hits a forehand down the line which draws B to the left side of her court and makes her hit a backhand return (1). The ball lands short in the center of A's court (2), so A moves toward it and hits a diagonal drop shot, for which B has to come racing diagonally across the court (3). B manages to get the ball back, but A then hits a deep lob over her head (4), forcing her to rush to the back of the court in a futile attempt to retrieve it (5). (Black stars indicate points at which players hit ball. Broken lines indicate movement of players. Solid lines indicate path of the ball. Encircled X indicates placement.)

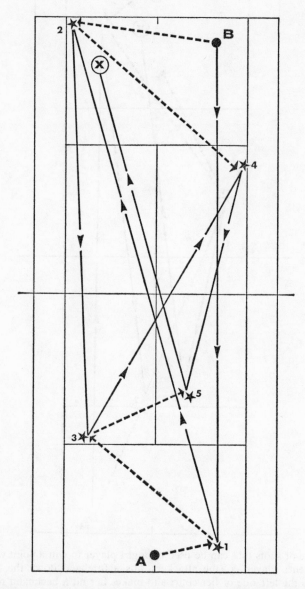

A second way to make your opponent run while winning the point: Player A returns B's drive crosscourt (1) and when B hits down the line (2), A hits a backhand crosscourt dropshot (3), forcing B to run up court. B makes the return (4) but is out of position and A hits an unreturnable forehand for the point (5).

In serving, you should try to keep the ball deep. Since most right-handed receivers play to their left to protect their backhands, frequent serves should be sent wide to their forehands in the hope of forcing errors. If the backhand is not thoroughly protected, aim the serve there, especially in the ad court.

If you have a good forehand, attack your opponent's serve at every opportunity, especially the second serve. Move over for the shot if you have to and hit deep to the corners, taking the offensive and running your opponent from side to side.

If you can volley and smash reasonably well, take the net after having placed one of your opponent's returns deep in a corner. Do not go to the net without proper preparation, however, as you will probably lose the point if you do. In moving forward aggressively when the opportunity presents itself, you will undoubtedly force your opponent to make a lot of errors simply by putting pressure on her. The more you go to the net, the more quickly you will develop this important element of the game and the more enjoyment you will get out of tennis.

If your opponent merely poops the ball back, content to win by slow attrition, change the pace of the game by mixing deep shots with short ones so that she must run up to the net and then chase back to the baseline. Again, if you have confidence in your net play, move in to the net.

Tactics against Left-Handers: Playing against a good left-hander can be a disturbing experience. You hit to what should be his weakness and it turns out to be his strength. You lob over his left shoulder and that is his favorite spot from which to smash. You hit to a big opening on what should be his backhand when he is at net and he reaches over with his forehand to put away the volley. Out of habit, you hit forehands down the line and backhands crosscourt—exactly what he wants you to hit. When he serves to the ad court, the ball pulls you far to your left, opening up the right side of your court for him to place the ball in.

What can you do about this? Everybody has to play against left-handers some of the time—there is no avoiding it—and since only about one in ten players is left-handed, their rarity gives them a big advantage when they play right-handers.

If you are going to play a left-hander, the most important thing to do is to *think tactics.* (Ideally, before you play a good left-hander, you should practice against one; but you can also practice against a right-hander and pretend he is left-handed.)

In both practice and the match, you should rearrange your thinking: hit crosscourt forehands and down-the-line backhands. (Most left-handers have strong forehands and weak backhands.)

Lob crosscourt on the forehand and down the line on the backhand. (This will put the lob over his right shoulder.)

Smash crosscourt—a natural shot for right-handers.

Serve to his backhand, especially in the deuce court. On this side he will be pulled out of court and you can hit the next shot deep to his forehand corner.

When receiving, remember that the spin on his slice serve will take the ball slightly to your left rather than to your right. However, you should stand about where you would to receive a right-hander's serve. If you stand too far to your left in order to protect your backhand, the server may ace you. In the ad court especially, you must expect to receive a lot of serves to your backhand. Concentrate on the toss, get ready in plenty of time, and be sure you keep the ball in play.

Aside to Left-Handers: If you have read the above, you can see some of the natural advantages you have in being left-handed—if you did not already know them. Because of these advantages, you should be an attacking player, capitalizing on your serve (particularly in the ad court) to assume the offensive. Your most effective shots will probably be crosscourt forehands, your serve, and crosscourt smashes—all aggressive strokes. Thus you should go to net as much as possible, volleying and smashing and putting pressure on your opponent.

Aside to Everybody: A great deal of the time (perhaps half the time) you are going to be pitted against a player stronger and

more experienced than yourself. Before you start playing, consider
the outside factors that may rebound to your advantage:

—Are you in better condition than he is?

—Are there any weather conditions—wind or sun—that you can
make use of?

—Is he overconfident and likely to drop a game or two before
he starts concentrating?

—Does he try less hard when he has a lead in games?

—Is he a thinking player, or can you outfox him if you use
all your tennis knowledge?

And if he does beat you, ask yourself when it is over: What
program should I follow to become better than he is?

CHAPTER TWELVE

Doubles: The Game and Its Tactics

Differences between Singles and Doubles: Doubles has a great many things in common with singles, but when the game is played correctly it requires vastly different strategems and skills. The two major distinctions between singles and doubles are (*a*) that doubles is a game of teamwork and (*b*)that the winning team is usually the one that plays best up at net.

A good singles player is not necessarily a good doubles player, and the reverse is also true. Everyone who watches tennis regularly is familiar with cases in which two superb singles players, teaming up for the first time, have been made to look foolish by a pair of less agile but more experienced doubles players. There are also many cases in which a team wins handily at first and then, through lack of harmony between the players, loses concentration and plunges to defeat.

Singles is primarily a game of making your opponent move around the court and of hitting shots that will force a weak return or an error; doubles, in its proper form, is a game of hitting shots that will enable you and your partner to establish yourselves at the net. Two players stationed at the net are much more effective than a single player at cutting off passing shots—even though the area to be covered is wider on the doubles court. Your opponents must make very good shots indeed to get the ball past you and still keep it within the boundaries of the court. Often their only recourse is to try to drive you back with lobs, which is why you see so much more lobbing (and smashing) in doubles than in singles.

The serving team, because it has a man already stationed at the net, holds a big advantage over the receiving team. Against alert opposition, if the receiver does not make a fast, low, crosscourt return, his side may lose the point. At the very top level of tennis, there are times when the serving team hardly ever loses a game, which results in marathon matches. One such match took place at Wimbledon in 1949. Four great servers and volleyers—Pancho Gonzalez and Hugh Stewart, Ted Schroeder and Bob Falkenburg— played a match that lasted five hours and twenty minutes. Schroeder and Falkenburg finally won, 36–34, 4–6, 3–6, 6–4, and 19–17.

Psychologically, too, singles and doubles are quite different. In singles, you rely on your own strokes, your will to win and depth of experience; in doubles you rely to a great extent on your partner—his understanding of doubles tactics, his ability to hit the right shot when it is called for, and his ability to stay calm under pressure.

A compatible partner is immensely valuable in doubles because of the amount of mental pressure involved. Shots must be more accurate in doubles. A PLACEMENT has to get past two players instead of only one and if both opponents are posted at the net, the shot can be volleyed away for the point unless it is very well hit. In addition, you have no control over the shots your partner makes, and he may lose your side a great many points by hitting weak shots or by making errors. In singles, a minor mistake can often be rectified by scrambling, by good anticipation or by lifting a desperate lob. In doubles, if your opponents post themselves at the net, they can put away most weak shots or force even weaker returns because a doubles team, with its extra player, can afford to be more aggressive than a person playing singles.

There is also the pressure you impose on yourself in doubles: you may worry about hitting a weak service return that the net man can pounce on; you may feel you are not giving your partner enough support; you may try extra hard on critical points and, because you are tense, make an error.

However, when you have played a good deal of doubles the

pressure lessens. You automatically hit shots to the right places. Realizing that your partner is trying his best, you merely determine to fight harder when he loses your side a point. The experienced player makes sure he does not give away easy points, encourages his partner, and tries to put pressure on his opponents.

The Doubles Partner: Part strategist and part diplomat, the good doubles player discusses the question of changing tactics with his partner; compliments his partner after the latter has made a good shot or has neatly set up a point; yells "Yours!" or "I've got it!" when there is doubt as to who should take a shot; lets his partner know, in plenty of time, when a ball hit by an opponent is going out; and is quick to assume the blame when he has hit a weak shot that has put his partner in jeopardy. He is also quick to cut off opponents' shots when they pass near him at the net and to move up to the net after a FORCING SHOT or a deep lob. He maintains his concentration in spite of all obstacles so that he will not miss easy shots or present setups to the opponents.

The ineffective doubles player, on the other hand, scowls at his partner when the latter misses a shot; hits a hard first serve that seldom goes in and a weak second serve; acts lazy or timid in not getting to the net after a forcing shot; panics when his opponents take the net; loses confidence and plays lackadaisically when his opponents have a commanding lead. A person with these habits, needless to say, is a consistent loser, is unpleasant to play with, and is not sought after as a partner.

Taking the Net: It is an axiom in doubles that, when a forcing shot has placed the opponents in a defensive position, two players at the net are much more valuable than one. This is because the two men present a greater threat of cutting off a weak shot by the opponents, thereby limiting the possibilities for an effective return. If the net players are alert and aggressive, only a low, fast, precisely aimed shot will get past them. Anything else can be cut off for a volleyed placement. The net players must, of course, be prepared for a lob, but the lob may be short, giving them an easy smash, or it may go out. Even if it is well-hit, it can be chased,

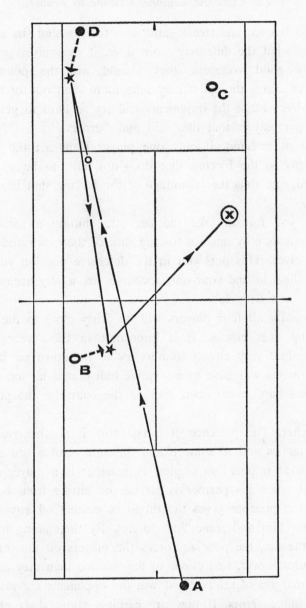

A useful poach: Server A hits a deep serve that Receiver D has difficulty with, hitting the return toward the middle instead of crosscourt. Net Man B attacks the ball by taking a step and reaching out on his forehand, putting the ball out of reach of C for the point. The likelihood of the net man successfully poaching puts great pressure on the receiver. (Small circle indicates bounce point of ball.)

allowed to bounce and struck hard as a forcing shot. In any event, no matter what the defensive team does, if the players at net are reasonably good volleyers, they should win the point in the majority of cases, though it may take more than one or two shots to do it. Very often the opponents will try so hard to get the ball past the net players that they will make errors.

On the other hand, if only one player is at net the defensive team's reply to the forcing shot does not have to be so accurate or so hard, and thus the advantage of the forcing shot is somewhat dispelled.

Should you fail to take the net after hitting a forcing shot, your opponents may make a forcing shot of their own and take the net themselves. This puts you in the defensive position you should have put them in and your only recourses are a very accurate PASS-ING SHOT or a deep lob.

Occasionally all four players will be fairly close to the net and a volleying duel ensues. It is important in these encounters to watch the ball very closely and to try to hit down on it so that your opponents will have to hit up. A ball that is hit too high can be returned hard to an open spot on the court for the point.

The Poacher: The presence of a POACHER is another reason why different tactics and to some extent different strokes are employed in doubles as opposed to singles. A poacher is a player stationed at the net when his partner is serving or hitting from backcourt, and an alert poacher poses the threat of cutting off any shot that comes near him and some that do not. By threatening to cut off shots at the net, the poacher forces the players on the other team to hit harder, lower, and closer to the sideline than they might like to. With margins of safety cut down, the opponents are much more likely to make errors. If they are careless about shots or if they are forced to hit weak ones, the poacher is often in a position to put them away.

Basic Doubles Strokes: Because of the emphasis on net play in doubles and the existence of the peripatetic poacher, a reasonably good doubles player should have the following shots at his command:

(1) A serve that goes in consistently. It does not have to be hard but it should be deep and well-placed so as to put the receiver on the defensive. The second serve should be nearly as hard as the first—but the first serve should go in most of the time. The receiving team has a marked advantage if the second serve is weak. A sharp return directed at the net man can put him in trouble and a hard crosscourt shot can allow the receiving team to take the offensive.

(2) A steady, well-placed return of serve. The return should be hit low and out of reach of the server's partner at the net. Above all, the receiver should try to keep the ball in play and not give the serving team any easy points.

(3) A good, consistent smash. Since there is more lobbing in doubles than singles, a reliable smash is essential. A player who smashes weakly or misses easy smashes is of little use to his team.

(4) A good lob. This is the desperation shot that can save the situation temporarily when you are on the defensive by giving you time to get back in position when you are out of court. If hit properly, a lob can force your opponents away from the net. If you can lob most of your opponents' smashes back, they are likely to start missing and you will pick up a good many points.

(5) Good passing shots off the forehand and backhand. These are used when your opponents have posted themselves at the net and are ready to pounce on your return. The shots should be kept low and should be hit crisply. They should be aimed for openings at the sides or down the middle. The shots do not have to be hard, and they should be hit with a slight amount of topspin. The spin makes the ball fly upward when an opponent volleys, and the higher his return is, the better chance you will have to get it back. If it is quite high, it can be hit down on for a placement.

(6) Good forcing shots. These are shots hit off balls that land at about the service line when the opponents are playing back. You should move in on the ball, take it at the top of its bounce and place it deep in your opponents' court. As one player moves forward to take the ball, his partner should go forward

with him. If the striker's partner lags behind, an opportunity to win the point may be lost.

(7) Fair ability to retrieve. This is not as important as it is in singles, but doubles players should be able to scramble around the court and get back sharply angled shots and hard smashes. Sometimes great defensive play by one team will blunt the opposing team's attack and force them, out of frustration or impatience, to start missing—after which the defenders can launch their own attack.

(8) An excellent volley. This is the *sine qua non* of doubles as the game is played today. A player who is reluctant to volley or who keeps missing volleys is a poor doubles player—and by the same token, a player who is deficient in many other respects but who volleys aggressively and seldom misses is a valuable partner to have.

One reason that good singles players do not necessarily make good doubles players is that they have developed patterns of play geared to defeating a lone opponent in a somewhat narrower court. For example, a down-the-line service return in the deuce court is a strong shot in singles. It cannot be used (except on rare occasions) in doubles because a net man is there to handle it. Also, a singles player may find that relatively slow groundstrokes, accurately and steadily hit, win him his share of matches. But with opponents standing at the net ready to intercept these shots, he must aim closer to the top of the net and hit a little bit harder to make volleying difficult. In singles, there are times when a drop shot is useful for winning a point or for tiring your opponent; in doubles, the shot pulls one opponent up to net—where he wants to be anyway—and, with his partner helping him cover the court, the fact that he may be pulled out of position is not as critical as in singles. As for the drop shot's other main purpose, there are so many chances to catch one's breath in doubles that fatigue should seldom be a factor. Finally, a singles player can be fairly careless about some shots when his opponent is in the back of the court; against a good doubles team, with the opponents at net, a careless shot is usually fatal.

Court Positions: Beginning players, naturally, have not yet developed the strokes, anticipation, or court sense to play doubles the way advanced players do. In the vast majority of cases, the beginner should not follow his serve to the net—as is recommended for players of experience. Beginners will miss a good many volleys while stationed at the net, and will also miss a good many smashes. In addition, the beginner may fail to cover a spot on the court that his partner has left open.

However, beginners should place themselves on the court in somewhat the same way as advanced doubles players. That is, the server should stand a little more to the right than in singles when serving to the deuce court, and to the left when serving to the ad court. This is so that he can cover the alleys on each side while his partner, at net, covers the other side of the court.

The net player on the serving team should play about a yard from the net, covering the alley. Advanced players stand farther back, where they can cover more territory, but volleying successfully this far from the net requires lots of practice. The closer you are to the net, the easier the volley is because you are hitting down at a sharp angle rather than at a shallow angle or, in some cases, upward. As you improve, you can stand farther back from the alley.

The player receiving the serve stands in the position he takes in singles, while his partner stations himself a little bit closer to the net—about halfway between the baseline and the rear service line. In advanced doubles the partner of the player receiving service stands quite close to the net. This is so that if his partner hits a strong return of service he is ready to cut off the serving team's answering shot. In most cases, this will be a low dipping shot that the server, running in, must volley upward. If the server's return is weak, the receiver's partner may be able to volley it away for the point. For beginners, the position of the receiver's partner is more of a defensive one. He must be ready to return a shot by the net man anywhere on his side of the court. He can do this most effectively if he stays farther back than would an advanced player—about three yards in from the baseline—although he must be ready to run forward to take a short ball on his side.

During rallies, both teams should be on the lookout for short shots that can be hit deep and followed in to the net. Both players should advance at the same time, presenting a solid wall to the opposition. If neither team advances to the net when opportunities arise, the game is not doubles but singles played by four people. While at first the volleyers may miss as many shots as they hit, they are playing the game properly in a tactical sense and gaining valuable experience for the future. As a very wise pro once remarked, "You have to miss before you can hit."

The Serving Team: This is traditionally the attacking team and is expected to win most of its games. The serving team has a big advantage over the receiving team and the reasons for this are the same, no matter what the level of tennis. The server puts the ball in play where the receiver will have the most trouble in returning it; and he has a helper up at net whose presence limits the number of places to which the receiver can safely return the ball. As the server starts the point, it is two against one. Unless the serve is a poor one or the receiver makes a fine return, the serving team, with these advantages, generally wins the point.

In serving to the deuce court against a right-hander, the server should almost always aim for the receiver's backhand. A serve to the forehand gives the receiver a chance to hit down the net man's alley and also gives him a good angle for crosscourt shots. In most cases, the backhand side will be the weaker one and the return will not be forcing. However, if the receiver plays far to his left to protect his backhand, then, of course, the serve should be directed wide to his forehand. In serving to a left-handed player in the deuce court (if the situation should arise) the server should aim wide to the left-hander's backhand.

In serving to the ad court against a right-hander, the server should also aim for the receiver's backhand in most cases. In addition to putting the ball on what is probably his weaker side, this pulls him out of court, leaving the middle open for a drive or volley. Again, if the receiver plays far to his left to protect his backhand, aim close to the line on his forehand side. Against a left-hander in the ad court (a relatively common situation), the server should again aim for the left-hander's backhand.

The server should make sure to get the first ball in, even at the sacrifice of some speed. On the second serve, the receiver will be filled with confidence; he may move in and hit a very strong return. There is also the danger of double-faulting—which brings joy to the opponents and dismay to one's partner.

After serving, take a step or two toward the net, ready to move in on a short ball or to return the receiver's shot as deep as is consistent with safety. If the receiver's partner is at net, the return must be hit crosscourt; hitting to a net man in the hope of catching him napping is usually suicidal. The server should also be ready to cover a lob over the net man's head. An experienced net man will quickly retreat and cover his own lobs, but in beginning doubles, net men are not always capable of racing back to make the smash. The server should be especially alert for this reply when serving to the deuce court, since he will have to take the lob on the backhand—sometimes a difficult shot. A smart pair of receivers will crowd the net after this shot, and the safest return is a crosscourt lob which may force them back.

If the service return is short, the server should hit it deep down the middle or to one corner or the other and take the net. Once there, he should be ready to volley the return or move back to smash a lob. In both smashing and volleying he should make sure of his shot, and not gamble on a winner. By keeping the ball in play and maintaining position at the net, he and his partner are putting pressure on the opponents. Because the defenders have to hit very good shots in order to win the point, they are likely to make errors or hit shots so weak that no risk is involved in making the PUTAWAY.

Since the server, being behind the net man, has a better view of the court, it is up to him to call, "Mine!" or "Yours!" in the case of lobs falling near the middle of the court. In most instances, the player on the left should take the shot if he can get into position because it will be on his forehand side.

When his partner is serving, the net man should be a tower of strength, since he poses the greatest threat to the receiver. He must of course cover his alley, but he should also be ready to dart over and cut off weak returns or move back to smash short lobs. The pressure he applies can be enormous. By his mere presence, he can force the receiver to drive the ball into the net, beyond the sideline or beyond the baseline in an attempt to keep the ball out of his reach. If the net man is successful in smashing lobs, he may force the receiver to lob out of court.

It is expected of the alert net man that he will poach when the opportunity offers—that is, outguess the receiver on some shots and, before the receiver has struck the ball, move to the spot he thinks it will go. It is usually advisable to let the server know when you are going to poach. This will enable him to cover the part of the court that you have vacated. If you and your partner find that your poaching is highly successful, you might use signals so that the server will know what part of the court to cover. A typical signal might be: as the server gets into position to serve, the net man turns around and faces him, putting his widespread fingers on his chest if he is going to poach, his fist there if he is going to maintain his position.

Of course, the poacher who consistently misses is a great source of anguish to his partner and of delight to his opponents. So if you find that you are making errors with your volleys or that your opponents' returns are hit too sharply for you to reach, you should play more conservative tennis.

The Receiving Team: The best shot for the receiver in the deuce court to make is deep and crosscourt. This keeps the ball away from the net man and puts pressure on the server. While it is inadvisable for beginning players to take the net on returns of service, both players should be alert to move in on short balls bouncing in front of the rear service line. When a short ball is sent over, both partners should advance to the net.

The receiver in the deuce court should watch for opportunities to hit the ball down the net man's alley. Some net players grow careless or move too far toward the middle of the court, anticipating a shot in that area. The down-the-line shot, particularly with the forehand, often wins a point and, even if it does not, it has the effect of keeping the net man honest.

A lob over the net man's head is often an effective shot,

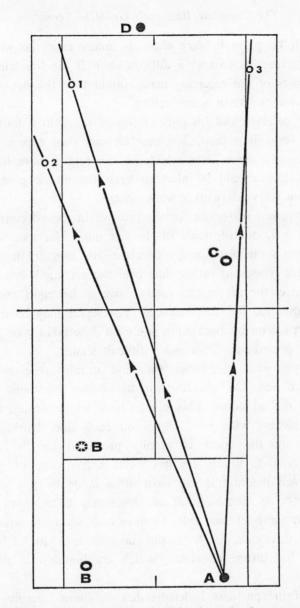

In doubles, the most effective returns of service from the deuce court: Receiver A's most effective shots are (1) deep to the server's forehand corner; (2) a sharply angled shot that will pull the server out of court for the return and leave an opening in the middle of his court; (3) a lob over the net man's head. In advanced tennis, the net man covers his own lobs, but among beginning players the server is usually obliged to rush over and take the shot on his backhand—which most players find quite difficult. C—Net Man; D—Server; B (black oval) —Receiver's Partner; B (broken oval)—Receiver's Partner if players are relatively advanced.

especially if he plays in very close. In many cases he will watch it sail by, giving his partner a difficult shot. If the lob lands deep, both members of the receiving team should take the net, ready to volley a drive or smash a lob return.

Both the receiver and his partner should move in a foot or two if the first serve is a fault. The receiver can then expect a some-what slower, shallower serve which he can return more forcefully, and his partner should be alert to keep the attack going if the serving team responds with a weak shot.

The best return of service for the receiver in the ad court is also a diagonal one, out of reach of the net man. He, too, may find down-the-line shots occasionally effective. His lobs are more effec-tive when hit crosscourt rather than over the net man's head. In the latter instance, the server can easily move to his right and hit an overhead after the ball has bounced. The server may have to take a crosscourt lob on his backhand, and even if he takes it on his fore-hand he is presented with a more difficult shot.

The player with the better forehand usually receives in the deuce court and the player with the better backhand usually receives in the ad court. This makes both wings strong, allowing crosscourt sweeps with good angles on each side. During rallies, the middle of the court is usually protected by the ad-court player's forehand, unless he has been driven out of position. Smashes down the middle are most often made by this player as well, since he is smashing off his forehand. Often both players wish to play the backhand side, because both want opportunities to smash. In this case, each should take a turn for a set and determine, for future reference, which combination is the more effective.

If one of the partners is left-handed, he should receive service in the advantage court. (It seems to be axiomatic that the fore-hands of left-handers are better than their backhands, even among players of top rank.) This is a very effective smashing combination since both sides of the court are covered and both smashers have good angles. Lobs down the middle of the court can be taken by the player in the better position. In volleying, since the middle of

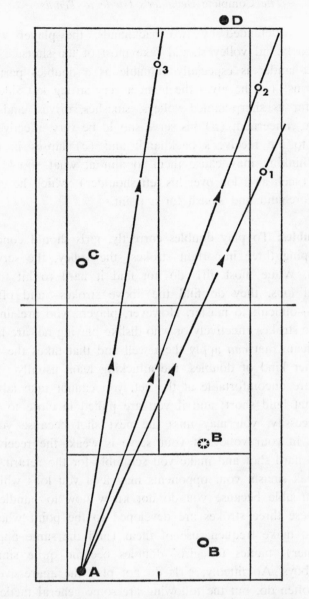

In doubles, the most effective returns of service from the ad court: Receiver A's most effective shots are (1) sharply crosscourt to the server's backhand, creating an opening in the middle of his court; (2) deep to his backhand, a shot which may force a weak return; (3) sharply hit past the net man down the middle, bringing the server to the middle of the court and leaving an opening on his backhand side. Another possible return is a lob deep to the backhand corner. A lob to the forehand corner is not a difficult shot for D to return unless he is taken completely by surprise.

the court is defended by two backhands, the player with the stronger backhand volley should take most of the shots.

The left-hander is especially valuable as a doubles partner for three reasons: (*a*) he gives the team a very strong left side of the court as far as sharp-angled volleys, smashes, drives, and service returns are concerned; (*b*) his serve should be very effective in the ad court to the receiver's backhand; and (*c*) lapses in the opponents' thinking may cause them to aim at what should be his weakness (such as a lob over his left shoulder), which he can take with his forehand and smash for a point.

Girls' Doubles: To play doubles correctly, girls should concentrate on developing three important strokes: the volley, the serve, and the smash. While most girls do not find it hard to hit forehand drives and lobs, they do find the above strokes—and often the backhand—difficult to master. However, players who are unable to apply these strokes effectively or who dislike playing net are likely to lose to a team that *can* apply them well and that takes the net. As in any other kind of doubles, the attacking team usually wins.

If you are uncomfortable at the net, you cannot take advantage of balls that land short; and if you are pulled in close to the net out of necessity, you may miss the next shot because you lack confidence in your volley. If your serve is weak, the receiver can hit back a hard shot and make you scramble for the return. If you have a weak smash, your opponents may feed you lobs which will give you trouble because you do not know how to handle them.

Once these three strokes are developed to the point where you feel free to make frequent use of them (and the same applies to your partner), tactics for girls' doubles become quite similar to those for boys. Admittedly, girls do not play the aggressive game that boys often do, but the following are some general tactical suggestions that will be useful if you are able to volley, serve, and smash with control and if you enthusiastically take advantage of your opportunities.

Serving: In both courts, try to place the ball on the receiver's backhand. If the receiver moves over to her left to protect this side, serve wide to her forehand. Concentrate on getting the first ball in so that you will not be in danger of double-faulting.

Be ready to return a lob that goes over your partner's head when she is at net, especially when serving to the deuce court. Unless it is an extremely short lob, your partner will probably let it go. After serving, be ready to move forward quickly to take a short crosscourt service return.

If your backhand is weak, protect it, when serving to the ad court, by standing just past the outside singles line. Be ready to move in fast for a short shot to your backhand, however, as this is a common and effective reply to the serve in this court.

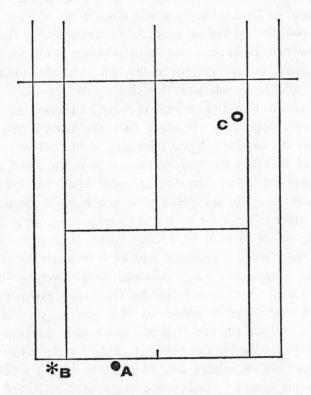

In girls' doubles, beginning players find themselves most vulnerable when serving to the ad court, because the receivers will almost invariably hit to their backhand. To protect the backhand, the server should stand very close to the doubles sideline. A—normal position; B—protecting backhand; C—net player.

Playing Net: No matter how uncomfortable you are at net, you are more valuable there than you are back at the baseline with the server and, with a little experience, you will soon find it fun to volley from this position. When your partner serves to the deuce court, stand astride the left singles sideline, about four feet from the net. The farther back you stand, the more difficult it is to volley. When your partner serves to the ad court, stand about two feet to the left of the right singles sideline; your forehand covers the alley more effectively on this side than your backhand does on the other.

During rallies, be sure to cover your own side of the court rather than move to the middle of the net. If you play in the middle, your partner will not know which side of the court she should cover and sometimes you will obscure her view.

When volleying, pay firm attention to fundamentals (keep your eye on the ball, maintain a very firm grip, get ready for the shot quickly, punch rather than stroke the ball) and aim most volleys down the middle—a safe shot that limits your opponents' possible angles of return. If you see a large opening, of course, aim for that.

When your opponents lob, move back the moment you see the ball rise in the air, even if you think that it will fall very short or that it will be taken by your partner. It is much easier to move forward and hit a lob than to scramble back for it, and the farther back you are, the better view you have of its trajectory. If your partner calls for the shot, make sure you get out of her way. If the lob comes to you, let it bounce, get your racket back in plenty of time, judge it carefully, and hit it in much the same way you would a serve—bringing the racket down over the ball and hitting it solidly. You should aim for the largest expanse of your opponent's court—that is, crosscourt when you are on one side or the other and down the middle if you smash near the center of the net. After you have hit the ball, get ready for the return, which will undoubtedly be another lob. If you keep hitting solidly, your opponents are bound to make an error, even if their first returns are successful.

If your partner should be forced to send up a lob that looks as though it will fall short, giving your opponents an opportunity to smash, move backward quickly to cover your half of the court, taking a position slightly in front of the baseline. When your partner hits a short lob, you are useless at the net and your team needs all the court coverage it can get.

Receiving Service: If your backhand is not as severe as your forehand, protect it by moving to your left. It is less dangerous for girls to do this than boys, since girls' services do not travel as fast and there is not as much chance of aces being hit to the forehand corner.

Keep the return out of reach of the net player and try to hit it deep. An occasional lob may give the server trouble, especially when you receive in the deuce court and can place it over the net player's head. If the net player stands or moves too close to the middle, hit the ball down her alley.

In the ad court, try to hit hard returns to the server's backhand. If the server plays far to your right and the net player stays close to the alley, hit down the middle. Occasionally a very short crosscourt return of service is effective, since this forces the server to run forward rapidly and scoop the ball up.

Rallying: Keep the ball deep and away from the net player. If you have confidence in your volleying, go up to the net when you or your partner has hit a deep drive. It is better if your partner accompanies you, but if she does not feel comfortable there, she should stay back. By establishing yourself at net, you have cut in half your opponents' possible replies and you may be putting a lot of pressure on them.

If a member of the opposing team shows a real weakness in handling lobs, give her plenty of chances to miss.

If your opponents have a tendency to hit short, play closer to the net—eight or ten feet in front of the baseline.

If one or both opponents play very close to the net, lob over their heads.

Mixed Doubles: This form of tennis can be played in two ways— for fun and for blood. In the social game, courtesy demands that the male partner hit easy shots to the girl across the net, saving the harder ones for the male player. If you are the male partner, don't hit tricky spins when sending the ball to your girl opponent and don't blast away at her when she is at net. Serve to her forehand, since this will probably be stronger than her backhand.

As far as your own partner is concerned, encourage her when she makes a good shot and commiserate with her when she misses. Let her decide which side of the court she wishes to play on— though it is conventional that the man plays the left side, since he usually has the stronger smash. The female player is generally allowed to serve first. In rallying, don't hog the court; let her have a fair share of the shots. If she does not wish to play net, encourage her to do so, but don't demand it. The longer that rallies continue, the more fun the girl players will have.

The girl player should do her best and not sink into despair when she misses a shot; there will be other opportunities to hit the ball. She should not, of course, criticize her partner's play or look upset if he double-faults twice in the same game.

From a tactical standpoint, here are some of the things she can do that will help her side:

(1) Hit to the girl opponent as much as possible except when she is at the net.

(2) If both opponents are at net, the safest tactic is to hit a lob.

(3) Play net on your partner's serve, even if you are not sure of your volleys; playing at the baseline gives the receiving team too much of an advantage.

(4) When serving, try very hard to win the point when you serve to the girl player; losing a single point to her may cost you the game.

When mixed doubles is played in dead earnest, courtesy and consideration go out the window. The male partner will attack the weaknesses of his girl opponent, just as her partner will attack the weaknesses of the female player on his side.

The following are some of the common weaknesses which male players can exploit to advantage. Girls generally do not hit slices and chops well; many of them are slow in running forward to retrieve short shots; it is often possible to roll around their services, taking the ball on your forehand side and hitting deep attacking crosscourt drives which force weak returns; they often have trouble with fast services to their backhands.

If the girl player has trouble returning hard shots, it is sometimes best to place her close to the net, covering one alley, while the male player chases all around the court hitting almost every shot. In self-defense, your male opponent may place *his* partner in a similar spot so as to do most of the shot-making himself. If he does, you should try to make him run a great deal by means of short shots, deep, wide shots and lobs over his head when he plays net. If he becomes tired, his accuracy will suffer. At the same time, you should urge your partner to try to put away all the shots that come within her reach. An alert girl net player can be a very powerful ally.

When your partner serves, do a lot of poaching, especially when the girl member of the opposing team receives. When you serve, concentrate hard on winning the point in the girl opponent's court; failing to do this may cost you the game.

If your partner has a good forehand, as many girl players do, encourage her to get into crosscourt duels with the girl on the other side of the net. You yourself should be at the net, ready to pounce on any weak return. Your presence there and the threat of having a return cut off puts pressure on the opposing players.

If the girl players are as good, or almost as good, as their male counterparts, the game can be played like conventional doubles and, of course, is just as much fun.

CHAPTER THIRTEEN

Practice

Importance of Practicing: There is a great deal to be said for intelligent practice. It can make a good player out of a fair one and a great one out of a good one. It can accelerate your rate of improvement. It can help you develop strength and endurance and can build confidence in your strokes. It is the quickest way, and sometimes the only way, to correct weaknesses.

Tennis history abounds with cases in which persistent practice dramatically helped players. Bill Talbert, the former American and Wimbledon doubles champion (with Gardnar Mulloy), used to hit balls against a brick wall for hours; then he would take a basket of balls and hit serves. As a result, although he started tennis relatively late in life, his strokes became "grooved," and his serve, hit with a minimum of effort, became one of the most dependable in the game. Jack Kramer, realizing the importance of the toss in serving, used to practice tosses in front of a mirror for long periods of time. Mike Sangster, former English champion, developed his powerful cannonball serve by practicing this stroke at least five hours a week.

Bobby Riggs, a good but not great player when he toured the Pacific during World War II, improved his game by practicing in matches. Instead of overwhelming his military opponents with his strongest shots, he allowed them to play his weaknesses. Under these circumstances, he had to struggle hard to win some of his matches, but after he finished the tour his game was much sounder. On his return to civilian life he played Don Budge for the world's professional title and scored a stunning upset.

Most tennis players would rather play sets than undertake the hard, sometimes tedious, work of a practice session. Playing is of course one way to improve; but it is tempting, in competition, to use only your best shots and to avoid using those that are weak. Thus as far as improvement is concerned, the time is largely wasted because your weaknesses are not corrected. Against a skilled opponent these weaknesses will be exposed and attacked, and in most cases this will mean defeat.

Correcting weaknesses is not merely a defensive measure. A well-balanced game allows you to make better use of your knowledge of tennis tactics. Often a player will see an opening but will lack sufficient confidence in his ability to hit the shot that is called for to make it. So he will hit cautiously, letting his opponent off the hook. Or he may try to make a placement and slap the ball into the net. Practice would have improved his ability to make the shot and, just as important, would have given him the confidence to do so.

Facing up to your stroke weaknesses is the first step in correcting them. Once you have done this, it is a good idea to consult a professional, a tennis coach, or a very good player. (Taking lessons from a pro is preferable, if that can be arranged.)

Even when a specific stroke weakness is spotted, however, it may be difficult to correct, and that is where practice comes in. You must hit a shot many times before all the elements fall into place—before all the proper moves become instinctive and your muscles do precisely what is desired of them.

That is why practices should be systematic. You should have in mind the particular shot, or shots, that need improving and concentrate on these. Most players limit themselves to working on three different strokes in a single practice session. This allows them to concentrate on the various elements of each and affords them the opportunity to hit the stroke over and over again so that it tends to become automatic and grooved.

Methods of Practicing: There will be times, of course, when you cannot find a partner or when you want to solve a particular stroking problem by yourself. That is when a backboard becomes extremely useful. Hitting balls against this indefatigable vertical wall will improve your timing, strengthen your wrist and forearm, and get you accustomed to preparing early for a stroke and hitting through the ball. There is no pressure on you to hit the ball where a partner can reach it and there are no distractions. You can concentrate on each element of the stroke—watching the ball, moving into position, and so on. In addition to that, the pure physical exercise is beneficial, since you are hitting many shots in a very short space of time.

Using a backboard allows you to practice the groundstrokes and—if you move in close—the volley. You can also practice the slice serve. You should not try to hit fast shots; hit the ball carefully, making sure you are developing the right habits.

For more accurately simulated competition, however, you should enlist the aid of a friend of about your ability and practice with him. At the beginning, simply hit the ball back and forth with him; the longer the rallies, the better. You can keep count of how many times the ball crosses the net or play "the game of errors," which was invented by Mercer Beasley. In this game players rally without trying to make placements, and each netted or out-of-bounds shot counts a point for the other player. The winner is the player who gets 21 points first. Incidentally, in rallying, you should always try to hit the ball on first bounce as in a game situation. Hitting a ball back involves getting to it, and this is as important an element of stroking as drawing the racket back.

Once you can hit the ball back and forth many times, try aiming all your shots for your opponent's backhand, and ask him to do the same for you. This will accustom you to hitting backhands of all sorts.

To practice the serve, you can play a game in which each player serves ten balls—five to each service box. The winner is the player who gets the most balls in. (The receiver hits the ball back, for his own practice, but no rallying takes place.) This can be repeated several times.

To practice volleying, one player stands at the net and volleys the groundstrokes his partner hits to him. No attempt is made to pass the net man, and the net man tries to volley the ball back so that the player hitting groundstrokes can keep the rally going. After ten minutes, the roles are reversed.

In another volleying drill both players stand at about the juncture of the rear service lines and the center service line. One player hits the ball softly over the net to start things off and both players volley thereafter, trying to keep the ball in play. This should be continued for about ten minutes.

To practice the smash, one player sends up a lob from the back of the court and the other player smashes. The player who is smashing hits where he pleases—to the corners or down the middle, wherever he can hit best. The player hitting lobs does not try to retrieve. After five minutes of this, the roles are reversed.

After both players have learned to smash with consistency, the lobbing player can practice retrieving smashes with lobs. The roles should be reversed after ten minutes.

Specific Drills: As you improve, you can try some more specialized drills, which will speed up your stroke development. Each of the following drills should be practiced for about ten minutes.

(1) Crosscourt forehand to crosscourt forehand, with both players trying to keep the ball deep.

(2) Down-the-line forehand to down-the-line backhand.

(3) Down-the-line backhand to down-the-line forehand.

(4) Crosscourt backhand to crosscourt backhand.

(5) Serve to the forehand and crosscourt return (in both service courts).

(6) Serve to the backhand and crosscourt return (in both service courts).

(7) For practicing approach shots: player A starts the rally, player B hits short; player A moves up to the ball and drives it deep to one corner or the other. Player B may then attempt to pass player A at the net.

After each practice workout, which should consume about a half-hour, the players should play a set to see if the drills have done any good and to determine what strokes need more attention in future workouts.

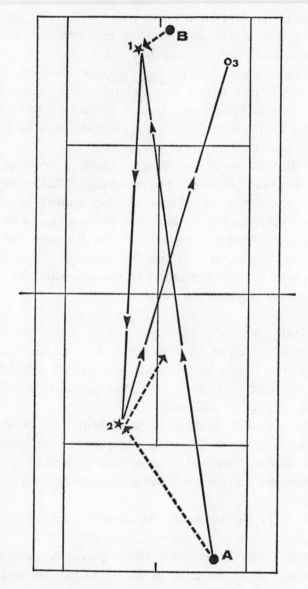

A simple approach shot drill: From the back of the court A hits a courtesy shot to B (1), who deliberately hits short (2). A aggressively moves in on the ball, hits a drive deep to B's backhand corner (3), and advances toward the net to cut off B's possible return. More advanced players will find it useful to have B try to pass A at the net after A has hit to the backhand corner, while A tries to make a putaway volley.

CHAPTER FOURTEEN

Conditioning

Importance of Conditioning: In this enlightened age of physical fitness, more and more athletes are following special exercise regimens to develop particular muscle groups and to increase suppleness and endurance.

To improve arm, shoulder, and back strength, Australian swimmers tie a large empty metal drum to their legs and swim dozens of laps. Some American high-jumpers do special isometric* exercises to develop their thigh muscles. Shot-putters, basketball players, wrestlers, fencers, and football players also take time out from practicing their particular sports to develop specific muscles. Experiments have shown that an athlete's rate of improvement rapidly accelerates with this type of program.

In tennis, the Australians follow a stricter regimen of exercise than any other nation—principally running, weight lifting, and special tennis drills—and their dominance of the sport shows how valuable this training is. At the top amateur level, moreover, their practice sessions are more grueling than those undertaken by any other nation. One consequence of this is that most top-class Australian players can play five sets (in the case of women, three

---

* An isometric exercise pits the exerciser's strength against an immovable object; he pushes or pulls as hard as he can for about six seconds and then, after resting for a second, repeats the exercise twice more. An isotonic exercise consists of repetitive movements against lighter resistance or no resistance at all. Calisthenics are examples of isotonic exercises.

sets) at close to full speed, and they usually win the long, tough tournament matches in international competition.

Being able to play at the top of his game throughout a match is the object of every serious tennis player, but one must be in extremely good physical condition to do it. What happens in the vast majority of cases is that a competitor plays at least three different types of tennis in the course of a single match.

First there is the feeling-out period, which may last for two or three games. The player has energy to burn but may be nervous or may find it difficult to concentrate on the match. He therefore hits relatively cautious, safe shots.

In the middle period, the player is warmed up, he knows what to expect from his opponent, and his shots are fairly well grooved. He finds the duel quite enjoyable. If he loses points, it is because of his opponent's skill, not his own mistakes.

Finally there comes the stage when weariness creeps in. The player feels the necessity of pacing himself. He finds he must make an extra effort to concentrate because his co-ordination has become a little bit wobbly. He is forced to play a conservative game for fear that he might throw away points. He may miss easy shots and grow angry with himself over his inability to bring his game up to its previous level. Small things—an idiosyncrasy of his opponent, a noise on a nearby court—may make him unreasonably angry. In extreme cases, his concentration and co-ordination may be so affected by fatigue that he puts up only token resistance.

There is nothing exceptional about this pattern. Almost every player is a little nervous before a match. As the match progresses, his strokes usually improve. Inevitably, as he gets tired, he will cover court a little less diligently and his accuracy will suffer. The important questions are: How long does it take him to reach his best game? How long can he apply pressure? Will fatigue affect him less than it does his opponent?

If two competitors are of equal strength and both are eager to win, tennis is a very taxing sport. Since the outcome of a match can sometimes be determined entirely by condition, it is clear that time should be set aside to do special exercises to develop endurance, strength, and speed. In fact, one tennis expert has said that a player with 5 per cent better condition can beat a player who is 25 per cent better than he is.

Endurance Exercises: Running is the quickest method to develop endurance. Long-distance running is useful for building up your legs and to some extent your wind, but wind for tennis—a stop-and-start game with brief intervals of rest—can be developed more quickly by repeated sprints of anywhere from twenty-five to fifty yards. Sprints put a greater demand on your lungs than long-distance running, and your lungs will soon begin to adjust to these demands.

Sprints develop speed and also condition the body to recover quickly so that a new all-out effort can be undertaken. It is important to develop the ability to make maximum use of the rest periods that occur after each point as well as the longer ones that occur when you and your opponent change courts after odd-numbered games.

The rest period between sprints can be from five to thirty seconds. Naturally, the less time spent recovering between sprints, the more quickly your lungs will develop. You should start with about five sprints and work up to as many as twenty.

For this type of conditioning, I recommend the purchase of a stopwatch. A stopwatch makes running more interesting because you can check your rate of improvement—by one-tenth of a second, if necessary. It also acts as a kind of indomitable task-master to make you try harder and is handy for finely timing rest periods between sprints. Keeping a written record of your accomplishments and noting your improvement will give you immense satisfaction.

Skipping rope is another good way to increase lung power. It can be done in various ways: skipping with your feet alternating in the kind of dance step used by prizefighters; hitting the floor simultaneously with both feet; hopping on one foot for a count of twenty-five and then hopping on the other; and skipping in reverse fashion, with the rope coming down over the back. You might start with about five minutes of rope skipping and gradually work up to ten minutes. If properly done, skipping rope can be as tiring as playing two hard sets of tennis. Again, it may be more interesting if a record is kept, with an eye to improving your performance—by even so little as five fast skips—every day.

Unfortunately in this country it is not considered lady-like for girls to run, except possibly when training for a track meet, although in almost every other country in the world running to get into condition for a particular sport is highly acceptable. Thus if a girl is serious about her tennis, skipping rope is an extremely useful substitute. However, since wind sprints are such a useful aid in increasing speed afoot and endurance, they should be done by the serious girl tennis player.

Stomach Exercises: Because of all the bending and twisting that a tennis player does, and because the stomach area is the source of much of the power in serving, smashing, and stroking, development of these muscles is as important to the tennis player as to the wrestler. Jack Kramer, when he was an active player, concentrated on getting three things into top shape: his grip, his legs, and his stomach.

(1) Lie down on your back, hands at sides, raise your legs to a vertical position and lower them again. Do this for approximately three minutes. Keep score and try to do at least one more leg raise the following day. To make it harder, after ten raises, halt the movement halfway up and halfway down for two seconds before completing the exercise.

(2) From the same position, raise your legs about a foot off the floor and flutter kick rapidly. Continue for about two minutes. Rest for a few seconds and repeat twice more.

(3) Lie down on your back with your hands behind your neck and rise to a sitting position. While rising, extend your arms so that they touch your toes. A slight bend of the knees may be necessary at first, but ideally the knees should be kept straight. Return to the original position and repeat about ten times. Keep score every day.

Leg and Thigh Exercises: (1) Assume a standing position, feet spread about twenty-four inches apart. Place your hands on your hips and go into a half squat. Hold for a second and rise to the original position. Repeat about twenty times. (Many authorities do not recommend full squats, as this places unwanted stress on portions of the knee. The "duckwalk" has all but disappeared as an exercise for football players.)

(2) Assume a standing position, feet spread about four feet apart, toes slightly out, hands on hips. Move your torso to the right by bending your right knee, keeping your body upright. Keep your left leg straight as your weight is placed on your right leg. After resuming the original position, bend your left knee and move your torso to the left. Do about twenty for each leg. This exercise is specifically for the leg muscles used in hitting forehand and backhand drives. If you wish to make it more difficult, place your hands behind your neck, spread your feet more and descend lower on each side.

(3) To do the exercise known as the straddle jump, stand at attention, hands at sides, then jump in the air, spreading your feet apart and snapping your arms overhead. As soon as your feet have landed in the spread-apart position, return to the original position and repeat the exercise about twenty-five times.

(4) Stand on the edge of a stair, weight supported on the balls of your feet and heels hanging over the edge. With one hand grasping the banister for balance, rise high on your toes and then sink as low on the balls of your feet as possible. Your knees should not be bent. Repeat about fifty times. This exercise will develop the muscles used for running and jumping.

(5) Do the same exercise with your knees bent throughout.

(6) Do the same exercise, not bending your knees, one leg at a time, for a count of ten; then do it with the other leg.

(7) The same as above, but with the knee bent.

Wrist, Finger, and Forearm Exercises: (1) Hold a light bar in both hands—palms up, a shoulder-width apart. (By light bar I mean the kind used to support weights; or a bar bell with ten-pound weights on each end.) Sit down on a chair or bench so that your feet are flat on the floor. Lean forward to allow your right hand, palm up, to hang over your right knee and your left hand, palm up, to hang over your left knee. The backs of your wrists are supported by your knees. Lower both hands simultaneously while grasping the bar, then, keeping your wrists stationary on the backs of your knees, raise your hands as high as you can. Repeat the up-and-down movements about twenty times. As your strength increases, repetitions should be added.

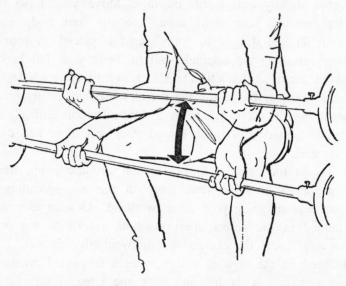

Repetition exercise with light weight to strengthen forearms, grip, and wrists.

(2) Hold a light dumbbell in your racket hand and, from a standing position, arm hanging at your side, rotate the weight as far as it will go to the right and then to the left. Repeat the rotary motion about twenty times. (*Note.* It is advisable, for reasons of physical symmetry and perhaps participation in other sports, to do this exercise with the non-racket-holding hand as well.)

(3) Squeezing a small rubber ball is an exercise done by many golfers and football players in their spare time—as when traveling on a plane or bus. Other athletes use a finger exerciser with resistance furnished by a coiled spring. These devices strengthen the fingers, wrists, and forearms—all of which are of vital importance in hitting tennis strokes.

(4) Place your palms together, as though in prayer. Keep your fingertips touching but move your palms apart. Press the fingertips

of your right hand against those of your left as hard as possible for a count of six; relax for one second; repeat the exercise twice more.

Back and Arm Exercises: (1) Push-ups, with weight on the palms of your hands, fingers outstretched and forward, and on your toes. (If this is too difficult at first, it may be more comfortable to support your weight on your knees instead of your toes.) The body is lowered until the chin touches the floor and then is brought back to the original position. After doing about eight, rest for a few seconds and do a few more. Once again, a record should be kept so that you can have a mark to break in subsequent sessions.

(2) From a horizontal bar high enough above your head for your hands to grasp it laterally, do five pull-ups, with the palms facing outward.

(3) With a light pulley weight, do the swimmer's crawl stroke and backstroke. Repeat each stroke about fifty times.

Suggested Conditioning Program: If you are playing tennis regularly, from twenty minutes to a half-hour of these exercises should be sufficient to keep your muscles well-toned and supple. The two most important areas are the stomach and the legs, and therefore the stomach exercises and wind sprints should take priority over the other exercises.

If you are unable to play much tennis, the exercises should be done at greater length and quite diligently. Here is a recommended series of exercises for those periods when you cannot get to a court. Altogether, with a one-minute rest period between exercises, they should take approximately an hour.

(1) Skipping rope (about five minutes).

(2) Leg raises (about three minutes).

(3) Flutter kick (about two minutes).

(4) Half squats (about three minutes).

(5) Alternating right and left knee bends (about two minutes).

(6) Five 50-yard wind sprints, if running space is available.

Otherwise, running hard in place with knees high for two minutes; rest a minute and repeat.

(7) Push-ups (about ten repetitions).

(8) Rotate dumbbell with arm hanging by your side (about twenty repetitions).

(9) Straddle jump (about twenty-five repetitions).

(10) Pull-ups (about five repetitions).

This routine is merely a suggestion. You may find substituting some of the isometric exercises more convenient, or you may feel that you are weak in one particular area and wish to concentrate on that. Again, it is an excellent idea to maintain a detailed record of the exercises you do so that you can keep track of your improvement.

If you can get to a gym in the months that you cannot play tennis, you will find the atmosphere conducive to vigorous exercise and all sorts of challenging equipment will be available.

It may take a good deal of self-discipline and will power to do the exercises described in this chapter with regularity, but the effort will certainly pay off in the development of a stronger tennis game. As one sage put it, when you're not practicing or training, somebody somewhere *is* practicing or training—and that man will beat you.

CHAPTER FIFTEEN

Preparing for a Match

General Preparations: The life's blood of tennis is competition, and every now and then you will be faced with an important match that you very much want to win or an opponent whom you particularly want to beat. Some of the preparations you can make are obvious: practicing to improve your best shots; correcting your weak shots; getting into top shape so that if all else fails you will be in better condition than your opponent toward the end of the match; and playing better players to improve your anticipation, speed afoot, and ability to concentrate.

Here are some additional steps you should take to enhance your chances:

(1) Watch your prospective opponent play and analyze his strengths and weaknesses.

(2) Practice beforehand on the court on which you will play, or on a court with a similar surface.

(3) Practice at the time of day for which your match is scheduled so that the angle of the sun will not surprise you.

(4) Practice against a player who plays the same type of game as your prospective opponent. Examples are: the player who gets everything back; the left-handed player; the player who hits everything hard; the player who puts a lot of spin on the ball and who frequently hits lobs and drop shots; the player who depends largely on his serve. While playing your simulated rival, consider how to attack his weaknesses with your best shots and how to protect your own weaknesses from his special strong points.

Warming Up: You can learn a great deal about playing conditions and the type of game your opponent plays if you are observant during your warm-up with him. Note the strength and direction of the wind and the angle of the sun. Is serving or smashing going to be affected by either? Also, study these facets of your opponent's game: Does he move quickly to get into position? Is he as strong on the backhand as he is on the forehand? Is he confident when he volleys? Is he sure of his smashes? Do his drives land short?

As far as your own shots are concerned, you should concentrate on fundamentals—watch the ball, prepare in plenty of time, swing through the ball, and make a conscious effort to relax. There is no pressure on you to hurry your shots and, at this point you do not have to hit with unfailing accuracy, though courtesy demands that you place the ball somewhere near the center of your opponent's court.

You should practice every shot—lobs, smashes, and volleys as well as drives. Ask your opponent to hit you a few lobs so that you can practice smashing. Just before play starts, you should hit about six serves into each court so that you will not double-fault or serve overcautiously for the first few points. If you are slow in grooving your shots, or if you need to work off tension before a match, it is a good idea to rally with a friend for a while, before the formal warm-up.

If you win the toss of the racket determining choice of side or service, you have a number of alternatives. If you feel that your opponent may not be sufficiently warmed up to serve well, it is a good idea to receive; you may score an early breakthrough. Or if you feel that the wind will be a factor and you want to make sure of the first game, you may wish to choose the court with the wind behind your back, keeping in mind, of course, that you change courts on odd-numbered games. You may also allow your opponent to choose first.

Equipment: It is not showing off but good common sense to bring two rackets with you, even if they are not of the same weight or make. (It is better, naturally, if they are identical.) The strings of one may break or the handle may grow slippery. Obviously, in such circumstances, a second racket is very useful.

Bring a clean towel for wiping your face, hands, and the racket handle; also bring a clean white handkerchief.

An extra shirt and extra socks may give you a lift after two hard sets if you have the chance to change.

Do not forget other basics, such as a brimmed hat or cap and a sweatband—inability to cope with the sun or perspiration on your hand can cost you some critical points.

Nourishment: On hot, humid days, some players find it helpful to take salt tablets before a match. These can be obtained at drugstores and at most tennis clubs.

To provide quick energy, orange slices, half-lemons, half-lumps of sugar, and teaspoonfuls of honey may be taken as courts are changed on odd-numbered games or between sets. However, carbonated beverages are not recommended during pauses in a match.

Needless to say, you should not eat a heavy meal just before stepping onto the court. The blood rushes to the stomach area to aid digestion and this is likely to cut your wind and make you lethargic. How much should be eaten before a match and how soon before it can be gauged only by experience; what is fine for one player may be disastrous for another.

CHAPTER SIXTEEN

Courtesy

Lawn tennis had its origins among the English aristocracy, and racket games in general were the delight of European royalty. For this reason, tennis comes to us surrounded by an aura of chivalric behavior and genteel manners.

One cannot imagine a pitcher saying to a batter, "Nice shot," as a line drive whistles past his ear; yet this is precisely what a tennis player is supposed to say in a similar situation. A tennis player is not supposed to argue with officials, as is traditional in baseball and basketball. In matches played without officials, a tennis player is expected to lean over backwards to make sure he is not taking advantage of his opponent. If something interferes with his opponent's shot, the tennis player asks if he would like to take it over. In most cases the opponent will decline—feeling that he might have missed anyway and not wishing to take advantage of another's courteous gesture. If a player is in doubt about a call on a shot made by his opponent, he is expected to call it good; his opponent, if he saw that it was clearly out, should overrule· him and call his own shot out.

Rules of proper conduct extend to spectators. They are expected to maintain a hushed silence during rallies so that players can concentrate. They applaud losers for a gallant try. They are not supposed to boo bad decisions—although they have been known to do so.

Tennis is, of course, played to win, and commendably so, but always within a framework of strict rules of conduct. Following the rules and observing the courtesies makes the game a great deal more enjoyable, since they are aimed at bringing out the better aspects of human nature. Here are the main rules of behavior that should be followed by everyone who steps onto a court:

While Playing: (1) Do not yell to an opponent across the net or talk loudly when people are playing on adjacent courts. You may interfere with their concentration, though they may be too courteous to mention it.

(2) Do not hog the court. Two sets are generally what local rules permit. The court should be relinquished without grumbling.

(3) Local rules often require that singles players double up if others are waiting. This, too, should be done at once and with good grace.

(4) If your opponent makes a good shot, do not berate yourself for letting the ball get by but give him credit and compliment his skill.

(5) If your opponent is about to wallop a setup, do not emit a sound of anguish or despair just before he hits the ball. This may throw off his timing, causing him to miss. It is most discourteous. In doubles, when a player has a setup, an opponent should not shout to his partner, "Watch your alley!" or some similar tactical instruction. This, too, whether it is intended to bother the hitter or not, is most discourteous.

(6) Never use profanity or slam your racket on the ground after missing an easy shot. These displays show a lack of emotional control which is disturbing to those around you. Besides, they may give your opponent extra confidence.

(7) Never interrupt a game in progress on an adjacent court to ask the players to send you back your tennis ball.

(8) If a ball belonging to other players comes onto your court, return it promptly without their having to ask you. Make sure you return it to the rightful owners.

Calls: (1) When you are playing a match with linesmen making the calls, do not argue if you disagree with a call. Assume that errors of judgment will even out over the match. The top players fully expect that in a long, hard match they will receive about six bad calls; but they know their opponent will receive about the same number.

(2) If you believe a bad call was made against your opponent, do not purposely throw away the next point to equalize matters. This is an ostentatious display of sportsmanship which your opponent and the gallery may appreciate but which officials will not. Presuming to overrule an official's decision amounts to a public rebuke and shows a lack of manners.

(3) When there are no officials and you do your own umpiring, call your opponent's shots accurately, honestly, at once, and loud enough for him to hear. If you have any doubt about whether a shot is good or bad, call it good. Do not play the point over; this penalizes your opponent for your failure to judge his ball. If it was impossible for you to see the ball, and your opponent was in position to see it clearly, ask him to make the call.

(4) Never call shots on your opponent's side of the court unless he specifically asks you to. Calling shots from afar will enrage most players.

(5) Assume that your opponent's calls are honest and that he believes yours are. Do not by word or look express doubt of his ability to make fair, accurate calls.

(6) Unless both you and your opponent have been playing tennis for a long time, the point score should be announced at least twice a game so that there will be no unpleasant surprises when one of you claims the game. Game scores should be announced after each game.

Serving: (1) Before serving, be sure to glance at your opponent to see if he is ready. Asking him if he is ready should not be necessary, however.

(2) In friendly matches, if the rhythm of your opponent's serve is upset by some distraction after he has served a fault, allow him two serves. For example, if a ball from a neighboring court rolls into your court after your opponent has served a fault, once the ball has been removed he should be allowed two serves.

Receiving: (1) If it can be avoided, do not hit back to the server first serves that land outside the service box.

(2) If a serve is out, call "Out!" clearly and immediately. If you call late, you may force your opponent to take several extra steps to hit your return back.

(3) After a point, return balls directly to the server. Do not make him scramble all over the court to collect them.

(4) If the serve is in and you play it, you do not have to call "Good!" Hitting it back will be enough. The same applies to other shots close to the lines.

Pregame Rallying: (1) In warm-up practice, hit balls deep and down the center of the court. Do not make your opponent scurry to retrieve them.

(2) When you take the net to practice volleys, hit the ball straight back to your opponent as much as possible.

(3) When your opponent is volleying, hit the ball where he can reach it; do not try to pass him.

(4) Allow your opponent equal time to volley and to practice other shots.

(5) When hitting overhead smashes, try for the most part to place the ball in the center of the court. However, a few smashes to the corners at the finish are permissible.

General Court Manners: (1) Before beginning play, note the kind of balls you are using and their distinguishing marks so that you won't get them mixed up with those belonging to players on adjacent courts.

(2) When a game is in progress, do not walk behind the players. If you must pass by, wait till the point is over and then move quickly.

(3) Do not talk to a player while he is playing a point. Between points, do not engage one of the players in a long conversation; his opponent may start fuming.

(4) Never deride a player for a bad shot or a mistake in tactical judgment.

(5) Do not expect your opponents to furnish the balls all the

time. After a while they will resent it. While you probably cannot afford to buy new balls with any great frequency, you should try to play with ones that have been used for only a few sets. Since the condition of the balls has an important bearing on the game, new ones or nearly new ones should occasionally be considered a justifiable extravagance. If balls are dead or discolored or too light in weight, the game loses much of its appeal.

(6) Traditionally, you are not supposed to ask a much better player to play with you; you are supposed to let *him* ask *you*. However, this nicety can be overdone. The way to rapid improvement is to learn how to handle the shots of more advanced players, and if the only way to enlist them is to make a frontal approach, make it. The request should be politely tendered, however, and if the advanced player declines, accept his refusal cheerfully.

(7) Never assume that because you happen to be a better tennis player than another person you have more rights than he has, or that you can be discourteous toward him because he does not have classic strokes. It is tempting to be extra polite to those players who can beat you and less polite to those whom you can dominate on the court. It is a tendency many of us have, unfortunately, but every player, regardless of ability, is deserving of equal courtesy.

GLOSSARY

ACE A service so fast or so sharply angled (or both) that the receiver cannot get his racket on the ball.

ADVANTAGE OR AD The score when one player has made a point after deuce. Advantage is "in" if the server wins it; "out" if the receiver wins it.

AD COURT The service court on the receiver's left.

ALLEY One of the two lanes, each 4½ feet wide, bordering the singles sidelines. They are used only in doubles.

AMERICAN TWIST A very advanced serve hit with sidespin and topspin. It causes the ball to kick up to the receiver's left after bouncing.

APPROACH SHOT A drive, hit deep, that can be followed to the net.

BACKCOURT The region of the court behind the rear service lines.

BACKHAND A stroke made on the left side of the body by right-handers, on the right side by left-handers.

BACKHAND COURT Same as AD COURT.

BACKSPIN Spin imparted by hitting the ball with a downward motion of the racket.

BASELINES The lines at each end of a tennis court.

BEVELS The diagonal sides of the racket handle.

CANNONBALL SERVE A hard-hit flat serve.

CHOP A stroke hit with backspin.

CENTER MARK The mark on the baseline that splits the line into equal halves to help the server establish his position.

CENTER SERVICE LINE The line separating the two service courts on each side of the net.

CONTINENTAL GRIP A grip in which the palm of the hand is farther over the handle than in the Eastern forehand (where the palm is behind the handle). This grip is used by many players for hitting slice serves and smashes.

DEUCE The score when each player has won three points; also when the player with the advantage loses the next point. A set in which both players have won at least five games is called a deuce set.

DEUCE COURT The service court on the receiver's right.

DINK A softly hit shot used by advanced players to bring an opponent toward the net and force him to hit up.

DOUBLE FAULT The situation when the server has hit two successive faults and as a consequence loses the point.

DOUBLES Tennis played with two on a side.

DOWN-THE-LINE SHOT A stroke hit close to and along the length of one of the sidelines.

DRIVE A stroke hit with a full sideward swing after the ball has bounced.

DROP SHOT A shot hit softly and with backspin—usually from the front part of the court—to make one's opponent dash quickly forward to retrieve the ball.

DROP VOLLEY A delicately hit volley that drops the ball just over the net—used mainly by advanced players.

EASTERN FOREHAND GRIP The most popular forehand grip. The palm of the hand is placed behind the handle for firm support and control.

EASTERN BACKHAND GRIP The most popular backhand grip. The palm of the hand is placed partly over the handle and the thumb is placed behind the handle for extra support.

ERROR An attempted return that goes out or into the net, or is missed completely, or is hit after the second bounce.

FAULT A serve that does not land in the proper service court; or a serve illegally struck, as when a foot-fault is made.

FIRST COURT Same as DEUCE COURT.

FLAT SERVE A serve hit hard and with little spin.

FOOT-FAULT An improper position of the feet before the ball is struck on the service, causing the server to be charged with a fault even if his serve lands in the proper service box.

FORCING SHOT A hard shot that requires one's opponent to hit a fairly weak return.

FORECOURT The region of the court in front of the service line.

FOREHAND A stroke made on the right side of the body by right-handers, on the left side by left-handers.

GAME A unit of scoring, six games usually ending a set.

GROUNDSTROKE Same as DRIVE.

HALF-VOLLEY A stroke made just as the ball comes up from the court.

HEAD That part of the racket surrounding the strings.

LET or LET SERVE A served ball that hits the net and drops into the proper service court. It must be played over.

LET POINT A point that must, for one reason or another, be played over.

LOB A ball lofted high in the air.

LOVE A scoring term meaning no points.

MATCH A competition between two or four players, usually consisting of two out of three sets and, with men, sometimes three out of five.

NETCORD SHOT A shot that touches the top of the net after the ball is in play and falls into the opponent's court. The opponent must play it as he would any shot that lands in his court.

OVERHEAD Same as SMASH.

OVERSPIN Same as TOPSPIN.

PASSING SHOT A drive that goes past the net player or players.

POACH To move quickly across the court in the area of the net and volley an opponent's shot.

PLACEMENT A shot that lands in the court out of reach of one's opponent.

PUTAWAY Similar to a placement—however, this term implies that the ball has been hit very hard.

RALLY To hit the ball back and forth in practice or during the playing of a point. Also used as a noun.

RECEIVER The player who receives the serve.

ROUGH Refers to the side of the racket with the slender strings *under* the gut.

SECOND COURT Same as AD COURT

SERVICE OR SERVE   The stroke that puts the ball in play at the beginning of each point.

SERVICE BOX   Same as SERVICE COURT.

SERVICE COURT   One of two courts on each side of the net into which the serve must be placed.

SERVICE LINE   The line twenty-one feet from the net in each player's court that bounds the rear of the service boxes.

SET   At least six games, though the winner must win by two. At 5-all, one player must win the next two games or the set continues until one player acquires a 2-game lead.

SETUP   A very easy shot—one that should be put away for the point.

SIDELINES   The lines on either side of the court that bound the playing area.

SIDESPIN   Spin imparted by bringing the racket strings across the ball sidewise.

SINGLES   Tennis played with one player on each side.

SLICE   A stroke hit with sidespin; but also a stroke hit with underspin, as a sliced lob or a sliced backhand.

SLICE SERVE   The most common serve, hit with sidespin for better control.

SMASH   A stroke in which the racket is brought down fast and hard on a lofted ball.

SMOOTH   Refers to the side of the racket with the slender strings *over* the gut.

THROAT   That part of the racket between the head and the handle.

TOPSPIN   Spin imparted by bringing the racket strings over the top of the ball.

TOSS   The "placing" of the ball in the air by the server before hitting the serve; or, before play, the spin of the racket to determine choice of court or serve.

UNDERSPIN   Same as Backspin.

VOLLEY   A shot in which the ball is hit before it bounces. Also used as a verb.

ABOUT THE AUTHOR

Rex Lardner started playing tennis at the age of nine and has been interested in all racket games ever since. He has written instructional material about tennis, squash, badminton, and platform tennis for *Sports Illustrated* magazine and has also written articles about famous tennis and squash players, and covered squash, squash tennis, badminton, and tennis tournaments.

Born in St. Paul, Minnesota, Mr. Lardner graduated from the University of Michigan in 1939 and served as a Signal Corps Intelligence officer during World War II. From 1946 to 1955 he was a staff writer for *The New Yorker* and subsequently became head comedy writer for the Ernie Kovacs show, winning a Sylvania Citation for Creative Television Writing and an Emmy nomination. From 1961 until 1965 he was on the staff of *Sports Illustrated*, for which he presently does free-lance work. He has written six books and has edited a collection of sports stories. His numerous magazine articles have appeared in such publications as *Esquire, Holiday, The Saturday Evening Post, Coronet,* and *The New York Times Magazine.* Mr. Lardner is married and has three children.